First World War
and Army of Occupation
War Diary
France, Belgium and Germany

55 DIVISION
165 Infantry Brigade,
Brigade Machine Gun Company
26 February 1916 - 28 February 1918

WO95/2927/3

The Naval & Military Press Ltd
www.nmarchive.com
Published in association with The National Archives

Published by

The Naval & Military Press Ltd

Unit 10 Ridgewood Industrial Park,
Uckfield, East Sussex,
TN22 5QE England
Tel: +44 (0) 1825 749494

www.naval-military-press.com

www.nmarchive.com

This diary has been reprinted in facsimile from the original. Any imperfections are inevitably reproduced and the quality may fall short of modern type and cartographic standards.

© Crown Copyright
Images reproduced by permission of The National Archives, London, England, 2015.

Contents

Document type	Place/Title	Date From	Date To
Heading	165th Machine Gun Coy Feb 1916-Feb 1918 Starts 26-2-16		
Heading	55th Division 165th Infy Bde 165th Machine Gun Corps Coy Feb 1916-Feb 1918		
War Diary		26/02/1916	07/05/1916
War Diary	In The Field	08/05/1916	28/06/1916
War Diary	Field	29/06/1916	30/06/1916
Heading	165th Brigade 55th Division 165th Brigade Machine Gun Company July 1916		
Heading	War Diary Of The 165th Inf. Bde Machine Gun Coy 55th (West Lancashire) Division For The Period 1st July 1916 To 31st July 1916		
War Diary	In The Field	01/07/1916	31/07/1916
Heading	165th Brigade 55th Division 165th Brigade Machine Gun Company August 1916 Account Of Operations Attached		
War Diary		01/08/1916	31/08/1916
Miscellaneous	Work Done During Operation at Maltz Horn Farm	16/08/1916	16/08/1916
Miscellaneous	165th Machine Gun Company	16/08/1916	16/08/1916
Heading	War Diary Of 165 Machine Gun Coy 1st September To 30th September 1916 Vol 8		
War Diary		01/09/1916	30/09/1916
Heading	War Diary Of 165th M.G. Coy For The Period 1st To 31st October 1916 Vol 9		
War Diary	In The Field	01/10/1916	31/10/1916
Heading	War Diary Of 165th Machine Gun Coy For Period November 1st To November 30th 1916 Vol 10		
War Diary	In The Field	01/11/1916	30/11/1916
Heading	War Diary Of The 165th M.G. Coy For The Period 1/1/17 To 31/1/17 Vol 12		
War Diary	Ypres Salient	01/01/1917	14/01/1917
War Diary	Ypres Salient VIII Corps Reserve Area	14/01/1917	31/01/1917
Operation(al) Order(s)	165th MG Coy Operation Orders No.3	30/12/1916	30/12/1916
Heading	War Diary Of 165th M.G Coy For The Period 1st To 28th February 1917 Vol 13		
War Diary		01/02/1917	28/02/1917
Heading	War Diary Of The 165th M.G. Coy for the Period 1st To 31st March 1917 Vol 14		
War Diary	Railway Wood Sector Ypres	01/03/1917	23/03/1917
War Diary	Railway Wood Sector	23/03/1917	31/03/1917
Heading	War Diary Of 165th M.G Coy For The Period 1st April To 30th April 1917 Vol 15		
War Diary	Ypres Salient	01/04/1917	30/04/1917
Operation(al) Order(s)	165th Machine Gun Company Operation Order No. 15	01/04/1917	01/04/1917
Heading	War Diary Of 165th M.G. Coy For The Period May 1st To 31st 1917 Vol 16		
War Diary	Ypres Salient (Railway Wood Sector)	01/05/1917	17/05/1917
War Diary	Poperinghe	17/05/1917	18/05/1917
War Diary	Watten Bollezeele	18/05/1917	18/05/1917
War Diary	Herzeele	18/05/1917	18/05/1917

Type	Description	Start	End
War Diary	Bollezeele	19/05/1917	31/05/1917
Operation(al) Order(s)	165th Machine Gun Company Operation Order No. 22	16/05/1917	16/05/1917
Operation(al) Order(s)	165th Machine Gun Company Operation Order No. 21	10/05/1917	10/05/1917
Operation(al) Order(s)	165th Machine Gun Company Operation Order No. 21	11/05/1917	11/05/1917
Miscellaneous	165th Machine Gun Company Appendix "A" To Operation Order No. 21	11/05/1917	11/05/1917
Heading	War Diary Of 165th M.G. Coy For The Period June 1st To June 30th 1917 Vol 17		
War Diary	Bollezeele (France)	01/06/1917	10/06/1917
War Diary	Ypres Salient	11/06/1917	23/06/1917
War Diary	Ypres Salient (Wieltje)	24/06/1917	01/07/1917
Operation(al) Order(s)	165th Machine Gun Coy Operation Order No. 24	23/06/1917	23/06/1917
Miscellaneous	165th Machine Gun Coy Operation Order No. 24	23/06/1917	23/06/1917
Map	Map		
Miscellaneous	165th Machine Gun Coy Operation Order No. 23	10/06/1917	10/06/1917
Map	Map		
Operation(al) Order(s)	165th Machine Gun Coy Operation Order No. 25	30/06/1917	30/06/1917
Miscellaneous	165th Machine Gun Coy Operation Order No. 25	30/06/1917	30/06/1917
Heading	War Diary Of The 165th M.G. Co For The Period 1st July To 31st July 1917 Vol 18		
Map	Map		
War Diary	Ypres Salient Wieltje Sector	01/07/1917	03/07/1917
War Diary	Brandhoek (Red Rose Camp)	03/07/1917	03/07/1917
War Diary	Zutove	04/07/1917	06/07/1917
War Diary	Botsdingaem Area	07/07/1917	21/07/1917
War Diary	Ypres Salient (between Weiltje And Potijeero)	21/07/1917	30/07/1917
War Diary	Ypres Salient (Weiltje-Warwick Fm Sector)	30/07/1917	31/07/1917
War Diary	Ypres Salient	31/07/1917	31/07/1917
Miscellaneous	165th Machine Gun Coy Operation Order No. 27 A	20/07/1917	20/07/1917
Operation(al) Order(s)	165th Machine Gun Coy Operation Order No. 28		
Operation(al) Order(s)	165th Machine Gun Company Operation Order No. 26	01/07/1917	01/07/1917
Miscellaneous	165th Machine Gun Coy Appendix A To Operation Order No. 28		
Miscellaneous	165th Machine Gun Company Operation Order No. 27	01/07/1917	01/07/1917
Miscellaneous	Programme Of Moves		
Miscellaneous			
Miscellaneous	M.G. Fire Organization Order		
Miscellaneous	Machine Gun Company		
Miscellaneous	Barrage Card		
Miscellaneous	M.G. Fire Organization Order		
Heading	War Diary Of 165th M.G. Coy For Period 1st To 31st August 1917 Vol 19		
War Diary	Ypres Salient (Wieltje Sector)	01/08/1917	04/08/1917
War Diary	Poperinghe	05/08/1917	31/08/1917
Heading	War Diary Of 165 M.G. Coy For Period 1/9/17-30/9/17 Vol 20		
War Diary	Nielles-Lez-Ardres	01/09/1917	15/09/1917
War Diary	Ypres Salient	15/09/1917	20/09/1917
War Diary	(Wieltje Sector)	20/09/1917	20/09/1917
War Diary	Ypres Salient	20/09/1917	22/09/1917
War Diary	Ypres Salient (Pommern Redoubt Sector)	22/09/1917	24/09/1917
War Diary	(Vlam No 2 Area)	24/09/1917	24/09/1917
War Diary	Watou No 2 Area	25/09/1917	25/09/1917
War Diary	Bapaume	26/09/1917	26/09/1917
War Diary	Barastre	30/09/1917	30/09/1917

Type	Description	Date From	Date To
Miscellaneous	165 Machine Gun Coy Amendment A To Operation Order No. 31	18/09/1917	18/09/1917
Operation(al) Order(s)	165th Machine Gun Company Operation Order No. 31	17/09/1917	17/09/1917
Operation(al) Order(s)	165th Machine Gun Company Operation Order No. 30	13/09/1917	13/09/1917
Map	Map		
Heading	War Diary Of 165th M.G.Coy For The Period 1st To 31st October 1917 Vol 21		
War Diary	Barastre	01/10/1917	01/10/1917
War Diary	Aizecourt	02/10/1917	02/10/1917
War Diary	Ste Emilie	02/10/1917	11/10/1917
War Diary	Epehy Sector	12/10/1917	22/10/1917
War Diary	Aizecourt-Le-Bas	23/10/1917	31/10/1917
Operation(al) Order(s)	165th Machine Gun Coy Operation Order No. 36	31/10/1917	31/10/1917
Operation(al) Order(s)	165th Machine Gun Coy Operation Order No. 35	21/10/1917	21/10/1917
Miscellaneous	165th Machine Gun Coy Amendment 'A' To Operation Order No. 34	11/10/1917	11/10/1917
Operation(al) Order(s)	165th Machine Gun Company Operation Order No. 34	11/10/1917	11/10/1917
Operation(al) Order(s)	165th Machine Gun Company Operation Order No. 33	08/10/1917	08/10/1917
Miscellaneous	Fire Programme Accompanying 165th Machine Gun Coy Operation Order No. 33	08/10/1917	08/10/1917
Miscellaneous	165th Machine Gun Coy Operation Order No 32	01/10/1917	01/10/1917
Heading	War Diary Of The 165th M.G. Coy For The Period 1st To 30th November 1917 Vol 22		
War Diary	Ste Emilie Somme Sheet 62c NE	01/11/1917	30/11/1917
Heading	War Diary Of The 165th Infantry Brigade For The Period 1st To 31st December 1917 Vol 23		
Map	Map		
War Diary	Somme Ste Emilie Sector	01/12/1917	06/12/1917
War Diary	Peronne	06/12/1917	08/12/1917
War Diary	Moroeuil	08/12/1917	14/12/1917
War Diary	Lisbourg	15/12/1917	31/12/1917
Miscellaneous			
Operation(al) Order(s)	165th Machine Gun Company Operation Order No. 40	05/12/1917	05/12/1917
Operation(al) Order(s)	165th Machine Gun Company Operation Order No. 39	18/11/1917	18/11/1917
Heading	War Diary Of 165th M.G. Coy For The Period 1st To 31st January 1918 Vol 24		
War Diary	Lisbourg	01/01/1918	01/01/1918
War Diary	Pas-De-Calais	31/01/1918	31/01/1918
Heading	War Diary Of The 165th M.G. Coy For The Period 1st To 28th Febry 1918 Vol 25		
War Diary	Lisbourg (Bomy Area)	01/02/1918	08/02/1918
War Diary	(Bomy Area) Cuhem	08/02/1918	09/02/1918
War Diary	(Busnes Area) Le Hamel	09/02/1918	12/02/1918
War Diary	Essars	12/02/1918	14/02/1918
War Diary	Festubert Givenchy Sector	14/02/1918	26/02/1918
War Diary	Essars	26/02/1918	27/02/1918
War Diary	Gorre	27/02/1918	28/02/1918
Operation(al) Order(s)	165th Machine Gun Coy Operation Order No. 42	25/02/1918	25/02/1918

165TH MACHINE GUN COY
FEB 1916 — FEB 1918

STARTS 26-2-16

55TH DIVISION
165TH INFY BDE

165TH MACHINE GUN COY
FEB 1916 - FEB 1918

WAR DIARY of 165th Bde MACHINE GUN SECTION
or INTELLIGENCE SUMMARY

Army Form C. 2118.

Place	Date	Hour	Summary of Events and Information	Remarks and references to Appendices
H₉	26/2/16		Machine Gun Company formed from the following Battalions 5th - 6th - 7th - 9th The "Kings" (Liverpool R.) T.F. The following are the details of the disposition of the Company in the trenches 4 guns in front line 2 guns in TERRITORIAL LINE 2 guns PETIT CHATEAU 2 guns WAILLY REDOUBT 2 guns PETIT MOULIN.	
	27/2/16		One Section + H/Qrs at BEAUMETZ. 3 remainder at MONCHIET (whilst the Brigade were in the trenches The Company was formed) The Section started duty in the following order. N° 1 Section (5th King) in reserve at BEAUMETZ. N° 2 " (6th ") in TERRITORIAL LINE + PETIT MOULIN N° 3 " (7th ") in WAILLY + PETIT CHATEAU N° 4 " (9th ") - FRONT LINE.	
	28/2/16 29/2/16		All quiet nothing to report	

CEubb Capt.
165th. Brigade.
M/G. Coy.

WAR DIARY 165th. Brigade
INTELLIGENCE SUMMARY M/G Coy

Army Form C. 2118.

Place	Date	Hour	Summary of Events and Information	Remarks and references to Appendices
	1/3/16		Guns were placed as follows from a position R 23 B 6-7 No I R 34 D 6.6 No II R 35 D 0.9 No III R 36 D 4.8 No IV R 36 B 5.4 No V R 30 D 9.1 No VI M 25 A 7.3 2nd wet fire was started 1000 rounds being fired	REF MAP FICHEUX 1/10000
	2/3/16		Relief took place. No I Section going in FRONT LINE all the Section moving on back. No II Section coming to BEAUMETZ 2nd wet fire 1000 rounds	
	3/3/16		Improvement of Old and M.G. emplacements + two new ones started in front line. 2nd wet fire 1000 rounds	
	4/3/16 5/3/16		Nothing to report all quiet on front 2nd wet fire 1000 rounds as usual.	
	6/3/16		Relief took place. No 2 Section going into front line next morning on own. No 8 Section to BIENVILLERS 2nd wet fire as usual	

Army Form C. 2118.

WAR DIARY
or
INTELLIGENCE SUMMARY
(Erase heading not required).

Place	Date	Hour	Summary of Events and Information	Remarks and references to Appendices
	7/3/16		Work on new emplacements in FRONT LINE & VILLAGE LINE	
	8/3/16		Nothing to report this week just as usual	
	9/3/16			
	10/3/16		Relief took place. No 3 Section to FRONT LINE relieved No 1 and No 4 Section to BEAUMETZ. This week just as usual.	
	11/3/16		Work on New emplacement, nothing to report.	
	12/3/16			
	13/3/16			
	14/3/16			
	15/3/16		Ins went fire on No 1 target of 6000 rounds, enemy to inform us seems no German working on Dugout. Relief took place. No 4 Section going into FRONT LINE & No 1 Section to BEAUMETZ.	
	16/3/16		Working parties on New trenches found at nights in German trenches, this week just fire around as usual.	
	17/3/16			
	18/3/16			
	19/3/16			
	20/3/16		New trenches in front have been finished & occupied. Relief took place. No 1 going to front line. No 2 Section to BEAUMETZ.	

Army Form C. 2118.

WAR DIARY
or
INTELLIGENCE SUMMARY
(Erase heading not required.)

Place	Date	Hour	Summary of Events and Information	Remarks and references to Appendices
	21/3/16 22/3/16 23/3/16		All quiet nothing to report. Manual M.G. not fire	
	24/3/16		Relief took place No 2 Section going into FRONT LINE No 3 Relief to BERLIMETZ. Manual M.G. not fire carried out.	
	26/3/16 27/3/16		Germans working parties found during these nights + expense M.G. not fire as usual.	
	28/3/16		H/Qrs moved from LE FERMONT to BEAUMETZ Relief took place No 3 Section moving into FRONT LINE No 4 Section to LE FERMONT. Nothing to report. Manual M.G. must fire carried out	
	29/3/16 30/3/16 31/3/16		All quiet nothing to report Manual M.G. not carried out	

O.Fill Capt.

165th. Brigade
M/G. Coy.

WAR DIARY

165th Brigade M/G. Coy.

INTELLIGENCE SUMMARY

Army Form C. 2118.

Date	Hour	Summary of Events and Information	Remarks
1/4/16 to 25/4/16		The following are the no. of guns kept in firing position throughout the month	

	1-5	5-9	9-13	13-17	17-21	21-25	25-29	29-3 May
FRONT MINE	4	1	2	3	4	1	2	4
PETIT CRATERS (4 guns)	3	4	1	3	4	1½	2	4
WRITE (2 guns)	3	4	1	2	3	4	2	4
PETIT MOULIN (2 guns)	2	3	4	1	2	3	4	2
TERRITORIAL MINE (3 guns)	2	3	4	1	2	3	4	2
FERMONT (4 guns)	1	2	3	4	1	2	3	1½ guns 3 guns

NOTE Numbers in squares means the number of the Section of the Coy. The Company were on the same Section of PETIT CRATERS. An Anti-Aircraft position was made at PETIT CRATERS but up to end of the month has not had a fight. The guns not in firing position are carried out on the usual precaution duty of 1000 rounds per day a very great march.

WAR DIARY
or
INTELLIGENCE SUMMARY
(Erase heading not required).

165th. Brigade,
M/G. Coy.

Army Form C. 2118.

Place	Date	Hour	Summary of Events and Information	Remarks and references to Appendices
	25/4/16		On this date our No 3 Section under the Command 2/Lieut ROBINSON took over three gun positions in the Right Sector of No 166 Brigade Front owing to their Machine Gun Company going out for rest + training. The manning of the Sections at LE FERMONT was then altered as No. Sections were able to go there, as all gun Sections were in the Line	
	20/4/16 to 30/4/16		Nothing to report. normal improving positions + adjusting which were carried out, also nil test fire as several Machine Guns were not called. During all the month the Machine Guns were not called on at all by the Infantry in the Line.	

Kelly
Capt
O/c 165th. Brigade,
M/G. Coy.

WAR DIARY
or
INTELLIGENCE SUMMARY

185th Brigade
M/G. Coy.

Army Form C. 2118

Place	Date	Hour	Summary of Events and Information	Remarks and references to Appendices
	1/5/16		Indirect fire carried out on RANSART, BLAIRVILLE + enemies trenches. No 3 Section attached to 166th Brigade machine shelled the district in FICHEUX.	REF MAP FICHEUX 1:10,000
	2/5/16		Germans opened fire of my left gun was kept in in fire on enemy working parties. Indirect fire on RANSART, QUARRY BLAIRVILLE WOOD + other points mainly Cros roads in neighbourhood - all quiet.	
	3/5/16		Reorganisation of place. No 1 Section relieving No 4 Section in PETIT CHATEAU + WAILLY. No 4 Section relieving No 2 at PETIT MOULIN + TERRITORIAL LINE. No 2 going into FRONT LINE No 3 Section still attached to 166th Bde. German Bombards made a raid on our Right. Indirect fire on German trenches North of RANSART + Cros Roads around FICHEUX, all quiet.	
	4/5/16		Took still going on but infantry on left quiet. all quiet 2nd west fire on QUARRY BLAIRVILLE WOOD + RANSART trenches, also fired at German trophies movement observed.)	
	5/5/16		No 3 Section attached on new implacement to 166 Tr Bay area. Indirect fire on Cros Roads around FICHEUX all quiet.	
	6/5/16		2nd west fire RANSART - TROISMAISONS - GRANCIS - QUARRY BLAIRVILLE WOOD Cros and Between BLAIRVILLE - FICHEUX, + FICHEUX all quiet	
	7/5/16		Indirect fire on Cros Roads around FICHEUX all quiet nothing to report	

Army Form C. 2118.

WAR DIARY
or
INTELLIGENCE SUMMARY

(Erase heading not required).

Instructions regarding War Diaries and Intelligence Summaries are contained in F. S. Regs., Part II, and the Staff Manual respectively. Title Pages will be prepared in manuscript.

Place	Date	Hour	Summary of Events and Information	Remarks and references to Appendices
IN the FIELD	1/9/16		Indirect fire on roads to FICHEUX + neighbouring tracks + trenches, no firing between 10 p.m. & 4 a.m. all quiet	REF. NAP (FICHEUX)
	2/9/16		Indirect fire on sunken road at R.3.d.10.70. PoMmeRcy at BLAIREVILLE + sunken road + trench at M.35.a.16. all quiet	1/C SE. TRIAS.W (Patrol)
	3/9/16		INDIRECT FIRE on QUARRY in CLAIRUILLE WOOD + on roads... FICHEUX & neighbouring Trenches all quiet	EDITION 2.6. 1. 16, 000
	4/9/16		No. 1 SECTION relieved No.4 in FRONT LINE, No.4 relieved No. 2 in PETIT CHATEAU + WAILLY KEEP. No.1 at MILLPOST + TERRITORIAL LINE. INDIRECT FIRE on BLAIREVILLE + QUARRY. all quiet	
			No.1 relieved No.1 at MILLPOST + TERRITORIAL LINE. INDIRECT FIRE on BLAIREVILLE + QUARRY. all quiet	
			INDIRECT FIRE on Trench + tracks at R.36.c.5.3, in Trench + trenches at Mer. Ia Rue town trenches at M.35.d. 10.60. all quiet.	
	5/9/16		INDIRECT FIRE on roads in FICHEUX VILLAGE + neighbouring trenches, all quiet.	
	6/9/16		COMPANY relieved by 166th BRIGADE M.G. Coys. The former taking over 2 left sections in FRONT LINE, LEFT PETIT CHATEAU + LEFT WAILLY KEEP positions + the latter 2 RIGHT positions in FRONT LINE, RIGHT MILL POST + LEFT WAILLY KEEP position. No.3 Section attached to 166 BRIGADE M.G. COY. relieved by that Coy.	
			COMPANY proceded to GOMY.	
	7/9/16		COMPANY arrived at GOMY 1-0 A.M.	

WAR DIARY
or
INTELLIGENCE SUMMARY

Army Form C. 2118.

Place	Date	Hour	Summary of Events and Information	Remarks and references to Appendices
IN THE FIELD	16/5/16 to 29/5/16		TRAINING at GOUY.	REF. MAP FICHEUX (TRENCH) SHC SE. 51b B 5W (part of) EDITION. 2t
	30/5/16		COMPANY left GOUY 7.3pm, & took up positions as follows:- No 3 Section in FRONT LINE; No 1. PETIT CHATEAU, "WALLY KEEP"; No 4 at MILL POST + TERRITORIAL LINE; No 2 in reserve at LE FERMONT. INDIRECT FIRE carried out by 166th BRIGADE on FICHEUX neighbouring Trenches.	
	31/5/16		New position at WALLY Pos. a & b, taken over by team of No 2 Section INDIRECT FIRE carried out on FICHEUX neighbouring Trenches + trenches BLAIREVILLE QUARRY; Sunken road at R.25.6.0.0; road, tracks, + trenches at R.26.a.5.8; Sunken Road + Trenches at M.15.d.1.6.	

Capt
for O/c 165th. Brigade M/G. Coy.

WAR DIARY
or
INTELLIGENCE SUMMARY

Army Form C. 2118.

Place	Date	Hour	Summary of Events and Information	Remarks and references to Appendices
In the Field	1/6/16	—	Nothing to report.	Refer: Map FICHEUX (French) 1/10,000.
	2/6/16		"	
	3/6/16		Cooperated in raiding scheme of 5th KINGS on enemy trenches near R.29.a.10.50 by indirect fire on communication trenches, roads, in rear trenches near by PICHOUR MILL & communication trench in R.35. From 1.20 a.m. Relief took place: No.2 relieved No.3. in FRONTLINE No.3. relieved No.1. in PETTICHATEAU No.4. — MILLPOST & TERRITORIAL LINE No.4.relieved No.2. as PETERMONT.	
	4/6/16		No.1. —	
	3/4/16 & 4/6/16		Nothing to report. Indirect fire was carried out from WAILLY/Frontline on the following targets:- Junction of roads + trenches at M.35.D.87.88, M.25.8.65.36, R.35.B.60.62, R.35.B.50.75, Crossroads R.35.B.50.75, Arch R.36.C.10.90, BLAIREVILLE QUARRY, Road + R.35.d.10.90, R.36.a.50.30, French R.25.d.94.60, road R.35 cd 80.30.	
	5/6/16		Nothing to report	
	6/6/16		do	
	7/6/16		do	
	8/6/16		Reliefs took place, No.4 relieved No.2 in FRONTLINE, No.2 relieved No.1. in PETITCHATEAU No.1. " " WAILLY. " 3 " MILLPOST & TERRITORIAL LINE, No.3. relieved No.4 at EFFERMONT.	
	9/6/16		Nothing to report.	
	10/6/16		"	
	11/6/16		Indirect as in previous week carried out each day and night.	
	5-11/6/16		Reliefs took place: No.1 relieved No.4 in FRONTLINE, No.4 relieved No.2 in PETITCHATEAU WAILLY	
	12/6/16		No.3 — LONG BARRA & PETITMOULIN No.3 relieved No.1 in TERRITORIAL LINE.	
	13/6/16		Nothing to report.	
	14/6/16		do	
	15/6/16		do	
	16/6/16		Reliefs took place. No.3 relieved No.1 FRONTLINE, No.1 relieved No.4 in PETITCHATEAU WAILLY 4 — 2 PETITMOULIN No.2 — No.3 in TERRITORIAL LINE	
	17/6/16		Nothing to report.	
	12/6/16 to 18/6/16		Indirect fire carried out on targets as in previous week — each day or night.	

BSD - B. M861 22/11. 12/15 5000.

WAR DIARY
INTELLIGENCE SUMMARY

165th Brigade M/G. Coy.

Army Form C. 2118.

Place	Date	Hour	Summary of Events and Information	Remarks and references to Appendices
In the Field	19/6/16		165 Infantry Brigade took up more line on right wing and including LINCOLNSHIRE SAP. No 2 Section took over from Off. Coy. 164 Inf. Bde. two new positions in FRONT LINE and huts in SUPPORT LINE. Remaining sections distributed as follows. No.1. 2guns PETIT CHATEAU, 2 MAILLY (Right) position & LONG BARN position. No.3. 4 guns FRONT LINE, No.4. 2guns TERRITORIAL LINE + 2 PETIT MOULIN. No. 4 Section relieved No. 3 in FRONT LINE (Right), No. 3 relieved No. 1 in PETIT CHATEAU + TERRITORIAL LINE.	FICHEUX (French) 1/10,000
	20/6/16		- relieve No.4 PETIT MOULIN + TERRITORIAL LINE. Nothing to report.	
	21/6/16		164 Infy. Brigade took over left of brigade line. No.4 position in FRONT LINE + PETIT CHATEAU guns relieved. Sections regrouped as follows. (1) FRONT LINE + Trench 190 MAXIM ST. & Trench 169 (SHORT ST.) 4 guns No 4 section (2) Ie. LIVERPOOL SAP ①, SUPPORT LINE 163/174 ①, TERRITORIAL LINE (left of) BREWERY ST.① No 2 section. BREWERY KEEP No 1 section. (3) CHEYNE ST ① TERRITORIAL LINE ② CHATEAU ST.② No 3 section (4) MAILLY ② PETIT MOULIN ② All quiet.	
	22/6/16		All quiet	
	23/6/16		Enemy front line from BRIGADE BATHS to S.A.P.C. kept under machine gun fire all night. 6 guns. I brought forward from reserve. Artillery carried out wire cutting on enemy's front throughout the day from R.34.c 40.40 to R.29.d. 05.50. 3 guns made kept under machine gun + Lewis gun fire on the and succeeding nights.	
	24/6/16		do on 24th	
	25/6/16		do	
	26/6/16			
	27/6/16			
	28/6/16		Bridging parties & division went over 5.20 pm: Indirect fire opened 5.5 am 6.0 m on trench (communication), Paths and no mans land between sunken road by FICHEUX and F.M. 25.b (communication trench) Retirement of raiding parties covered by front line guns. Discharge of gas carried by front line guns. 9 ups on enemy wire. kept open by front line guns during night.	

Army Form C. 2118.

WAR DIARY
or
INTELLIGENCE SUMMARY
(Erase heading not required.)

Place	Date	Hour	Summary of Events and Information	Remarks and references to Appendices
	29/6/16		No 3 relieves No 4 in group 1. No 4 relieved No 2 in group 2, No 2 relieved No 1 in group 3. Gaps in enemy wire kept open during darkness by front line guns. Nothing further to do.	
	30/6/16		K reports train carried out on BLAIREVILLE, QUARRY Roads in FICHEUX &	

Challis
Capt
of
165th. Brigade,
M/G. Coy.

165th Brigade
55th Division.

165th BRIGADE MACHINE GUN COMPANY

JULY 1 9 1 6

Vol 6

War Diary
of the
165th Inf. Bde. Machine Gun Coy,
55th (West Lancashire) Division.
for the period
1st July, 1916 to 31st July, 1916.

WAR DIARY or INTELLIGENCE SUMMARY

Army Form C. 2118

Place	Date	Hour	Summary of Events and Information	Remarks and references to Appendices
In the field	1/7/16		Nothing to report	
	2/7/16		Enemy bombarded WATTY and front line trenches near TITE STREET at 1 to 4 p.m.	
	3/4/16		Nothing to report	
	4/7/16		do	
	5/7/16		The following reliefs took place:- No 1 Section relieved No 3 Section in Group 1, No 3 relieved No 2 in Group 2, No 2 relieved No 4 in Group 3, No 4 relieved No 4 in Group 4. All quiet. Nothing to report.	
	6/7/16		do	
	7/7/16		do	
	8/7/16		Enemy's wire cut & cleaning parties in work on gaps made in enemy's wire by artillery. Indirect fire carried out during day & night on BLAIREVILLE QUARRY, roads tracks and trenches round FICHEUX and communication trenches to behind enemy lines facing Brigade front. All quiet. Nothing to report	
	9/7/16		do at night	
	10/7/16		do	
	11/7/16		do	
	12/7/16		The following reliefs took place: No 2 Section relieved No 1 in Group 1, No 4 relieved No 3 in Group 2, No 3 relieved No 4 in Group 3, No 1 relieved No 2 in Group 4. All quiet. Nothing to report.	
	13/7/16		Previous enemy working parties repairing wire dispersed by a/gun fire. An artillery combat. Amount of enemy wire from N to midnight 13/14/5 1011am and from 3-4 am machine guns co-operated from VILLAGE LINE both with indirect fire on enemy communication trenches, roads in rear of line opposite Brigade front. BREWERY POST, TERRITORIAL LINE (BREWERY ST), EARWHOLES etc. relieved by No 4 m/g Coy. 7pm. Relieved guns proceeded to billets at LE FERMONT.	
	14/7/16		Nothing to report. Fire carried out during two new works on gaps made in enemy wire by artillery. Harold indirect fire on enemy trenches to extend and dug & night. Brigade front extended past CUSTARD ST, guns at PETIT CHATEAUX and FRONT LINE relieved by this company.	
	15/7/16		Nothing to report	
	16/7/16		do	
	17/7/16		do	
	18/7/16		Usual indirect fire on enemy positions & gaps in his wire kept under fire all day	
	19/7/16			

(B 11384) W M B531 22/11 12/15 5000.

Army Form C. 2118

WAR DIARY or INTELLIGENCE SUMMARY

(Erase heading not required).

Instructions regarding War Diaries and Intelligence Summaries are contained in F. S. Regs., Part II, and the Staff Manual respectively. Title Pages will be prepared in manuscript.

Place	Date	Hour	Summary of Events and Information	Remarks and references to Appendices
In the field	20/7/16		M.guns relieved I/m. by 34th Brigade M/gun Coy. Company proceeded to BEAUMETZ	
	21/7/16		Proceeded to BARLY. 5/pm.	
	22/7/16		Proceeded to HALLOY. 7 am.	
	23/7/16		Proceeded to AUTHEUX. 8 am.	
	25/7/16		Transport proceeded to CARDONETTE L'ABBÉ	
	26/7/16		do MERICOURT. Sections entrained and proceeded to MERICOURT L'ABBÉ.	
	27/7/16		At MERICOURT L'ABBÉ	
	29/7/16		Proceeded to CITADEL (FRICOURT) BOIS DES TAILLES (MORLANCOURT)	
	28/7/16		At CITADEL BOIS DES TAILLES	
	30/7/16		Proceeded to CITADEL (FRICOURT)	
	31/7/16		At CITADEL (FRICOURT)	

Ashburner Capt.
for O. 165th.
M/G. Coy.

1/8/16

165th Brigade.
55th Division

165th BRIGADE MACHINE GUN COMPANY

AUGUST 1 9 1 6

Account of Operations attached.

Army Form C. 2118.

WAR DIARY
or
INTELLIGENCE SUMMARY
(Erase heading not required).

Instructions regarding War Diaries and Intelligence Summaries are contained in F.S. Regs., Part II, and the Staff Manual respectively. Title Pages will be prepared in manuscript.

Place	Date	Hour	Summary of Events and Information	Remarks and references to Appendices
	1/8/16		In bivouac west of BRONFAY FARM. Training carried out	
	2/8/16		do	
	3/8/16		do	
	4/8/16		Positions at DUBLIN TRENCH.	
	5/8/16	p.m.	1 & 2 sections relieved 2 sections 154th M.Coy in Front Line.	
	6/8/16		Whole company moved forward to MALTZ HORN FARM Trenches	
	7/8/16		1 & 2 sections moved forward to Nos 1 & 2 sections moved up & positions in COCHRANE ALLEY. No 3 Section advanced with 5th KING'S in attack movement of line forward.	
	8/8/16	a.m.	2 guns of section forward with attack by 7th KING'S. 1 gun moved with bombers took up position to cover advance by 9th KING'S. No 3. section relieved No 2 section in OWEN'S TRENCH. No 3 took up positions in advance of Front Line to support attack by 9th KINGS on isolated enemy trench.	
	9/8/16	a.m.	9th KINGS attacked covered by machinegun fire, and retired. Section support reported that he heard the order "Retire!" given.	
	10/8/16		Nothing to report	
	11/8/16			
	12/8/16			
	13/8/16	p.m.	Relieved by 166 M.G.Coy. & returned to bivouac near BRONFAY FARM	
	14/8/16		Moved to bivouac at VILLE SUR ANCRE.	
	15/8/16	p.m.	Inspection by G.O.C. Division	
	16/8/16		Training carried out	
	17/8/16		do	
	18/8/16		do	
	19/8/16	p.m.	Company entrained for CERISY GAILLY.	
	20/8/16		Training at CERISY GAILLY	
	29/8/16			
	30/8/16		Company entrained for DERNANCOURT.	
	31/8/16		Training carried out	

Hepburn Capt
o/c 166th
M.G. Coy.

MACHINE GUN COY.
165th
No.......
Date... 16/8/16

Work done during operations at MALTZ HORN FARM.

Machine Gun Company endeavoured to co-operate with Infantry & French Mortar Battery during the whole of this period.

Flanks of Brigade front covered by Machine Guns. Support trenches held by Machine Guns & reserve guns placed in support ready to move forward. Ammunition, water, & ration dumps formed with Reserve guns in case it was impossible to bring forward stores during the period the Brigade was in action.

Guns went forward with the Infantry, to cover them from counter-attacks when digging themselves in.

Guns went forward on one occasion to cover the advancing Infantry, more might have been done on this occasion by the guns, if the bombing parties had gone forward earlier, & guns established before Infantry advanced.

All information sent back was immediately given to Battalion Commander.

Y.S. Payne
Capt
O/C 165th.
M/G. Coy.

165th Machine Gun Company.

Work done during operations at MALTZ HORN FARM.

Machine Gun Company endeavoured to co-operate with Infantry and Trench Mortar Battery during the whole of this period.
Flanks of Brigade front covered by Machine Guns. Support Trenches held by Machine Guns and reserve guns placed in support ready to move forward. Ammunition, water, and ration dumps formed with Reserve Guns in case it was impossible to bring forward stores during the period the Brigade was in action. Guns went forward with the Infantry to cover them from counter-attacks when digging themselves in.
Guns went forward on one occasion to cover the advancing infantry, more might have been done on this occasion by the Guns, if the bombing parties had gone forward earlier, and guns established before Infantry advanced.
All information sent back was immediately given to Battalion Commander.

(sd) F.S.PAYNE. Capt.,

16/8/16.   165 M.G.Company.

War Diary

of

165 Machine Gun Coy.

1st September to 30th September 1916

Vol 8

WAR DIARY or INTELLIGENCE SUMMARY

Army Form C. 2118.

Place	Date	Hour	Summary of Events and Information	Remarks and references to Appendices
	1/9/16		Company at DORNANCOURT. Training - musketry - emplacements &c.	
	2/9/16		" " " Field work.	
	3/9/16		" " " Through the day.	
	4/9/16		Relieved 93rd Company. M. Gun in Line. Altogether High Wood & LONGUEVAL. Enemy Quiet.	
	5/9/16		Enemy kept down from all sides. My Machine Gun fire from SAVOY TR.	
	6/9/16		Unsuccessful attack by 6th KINGS on STRONG PT in WOOD LANE. Enemy hundred out on WORCESTER TR. Gun teams Brunel, Pte Price.	
	7/9/16		Acted m.g. for heavy bombardment stopped out Sgt Rowlinson.	
	8/9/16	P.M	Attack by LEFT BRIGADE on HIGH WOOD & supported by Machine Gun fire from SAVOY TR.	
			Attack on WOOD LANE by LEFT BRIGADE & 5th KINGS. GUNS in WORCESTER & TEA TRENCHES accounted for many of the flying enemy. Artillery active throughout the day. Ten trench shelters & men hurt but no action both shrapnel - Casualties 3.	
	9/9/16		Relieved during night by Newfoundland M.G. Coy - marched into bivouacs S. of FRICOURT.	
	10/9/16		Marched to GUIDE SUR ANCRE en route.	
	11/9/16	a.m	Reorganising & Section work.	
	12/9/16		General Drill & field work. Range practice - platoon practice. Examining trench work in conjunction with battalions.	
	13/9/16	p.m	Marched to bivouacs near BERTRANCOURT. Inspected by Brigadier General.	
	14/9/16	p.m	Marched to bivouacs at FLEURS relieved 6th M.G. Coy. - Weather very wet - Enemy quiet.	
	15/9/16	p.m	Relieved by 16th M.G.Coy, went into support at YORK TRENCH.	
	16/9/16	a.m	Attacked GIRD & regiment - Enemy Guns. Weather wet.	
	17/9/16	a.m	Relieved by 3rd M.G.Coy & marched to bivouacs on BRITISH REDOUBT.	
	18/9/16		General Company reserve - in reorganisation by Brigade General & overhaul of M Guns into battery posts.	
	19/9/16		Company training.	
	20/9/16		Marched into bivouacs in front of FLEURS & relieved 16th M.G.Coy.	
	21/9/16	p.m	Our artillery active - enemy quiet.	
	22/9/16	p.m	Continued attack on GUEDECOURT. 12 guns brought into action. 3 got position - all others knocked up & lost within our camp to Battery support of our division - one attack on advance of artillery to GUEDECOURT - right flank.	
	23/9/16	a.m	Barrage - Gun into the post. Barrage on GUEDECOURT. Night flank - enemy forces to advance in GIRD TRENCH when YORK TRENCH - gap heavy shell. Enemy quiet. Pushing enemy on mfg. 12 Z GUEDECOURT disposed of.	
	24/9/16	p.m	Relieved by 1st M.G.Coy. & sent into reserve in ration Trench 4th.	
	25/9/16		GIRD TRENCH W. of GUEDECOURT. Objective reached.	
	26/9/16	p.m	Enemy artillery active - Counter battery activity - no response. Enemy ammo dump near LE TRANSLOY.	
	27/9/16	p.m	Relieved by 13th M.G.Coy. Went into bivouac at POMMIER REDOUBT.	
	28/9/16			
	29/9/16			
	30/9/16		Marched to billets at BUIRE SUR CORBIE	

Capt.
O/C 14 M.G. Coy.

CONFIDENTIAL

Vol 9

War Diary
of
165th M.G. Coy
for the period
1st to 31st October 1916

WAR DIARY
or
INTELLIGENCE SUMMARY

(Erase heading not required.)

Army Form C. 2118

Instructions regarding War Diaries and Intelligence Summaries are contained in F.S. Regs, Part II. and the Staff Manual respectively. Title Pages will be prepared in manuscript.

Place	Date	Hour	Summary of Events and Information	Remarks and references to Appendices
In Field	1/10/16	a/n	Left BUIRE SOUS CORBIE & entrained at MERICOURT - arrived & detrained at LONGPRE & marched to COUQUELETTE	
	2/10/16	a/n	Entrained PONT REMY & detrained	
	3/10/16	a/n	at ESQUELBECQ - marched to billets at HERZEELE	
	4/10/16		Entrained at HOPOUDT & detrained at POPERINGHE - billeted	
		p.m	55th M.G.Coy in RAILWAY WOOD & POTIJZE SECTORS	
	5/10/16		Enemy quiet. Several reconnaissances of line. Jobs for alarm.	
	6/10/16		Enemy active	
	7/10/16		Enemy quiet. Indirect fire started on RUPPRECHT FARM	
	8/10/16			
	9/10/16			
	10/10/16			
	11/10/16		Enemy quiet. Indirect fire on VERLORENHOEK WESTHOEK	
	12/10/16		Our aeroplanes active	
	13/10/16			
	14/10/16			
	15/10/16		Enemy quiet. Indirect fire of M.Guns carried out daily. Enemy reply feeble forward.	
	16/10/16		Relieved by 164 M.G.Coy & went into huts at BRANDHOEK.	
	17/10/16		Company in divisional reserve - General training. Returned to lines and billets in reserve.	
	18/10/16		Brigade Inspection by Lt-Genl Humbersten. G.O.C. XIII Corps	
	19/10/16		Brigade Inspection by Brig Genl Duncan. Recreation & games between J.M.G.A. Teams. Relieved	
	20/10/16		Relieved 164 M.G.Coy in RAILWAY WOOD & POTIJZE SECTORS	
	22/10/16		Enemy quiet. Indirect fire directed on HOOGE & VERLORENHOEK	
	23/10/16		" " " " "	
	24/10/16		Enemy quiet.	
	25/10/16		" " Indirect fire during night	
	26/10/16		" " " " "	
	27/10/16		" " " " "	
	28/10/16	p.m	Our artilling very active	
	29/10/16	p.m	" " " "	
	30/10/16	p.m	" " " "	
	31/10/16		Enemy quiet. Our Aeroplanes active	

CONFIDENTIAL

Vol 10

War Diary

of

165th Machine Gun Bn.

for period November 1st to November 30th 1916

Army Form C. 2118

WAR DIARY
or
INTELLIGENCE SUMMARY
(Erase heading not required.)

Instructions regarding War Diaries and Intelligence Summaries are contained in F.S. Regs., Part II. and the Staff Manual respectively. Title Pages will be prepared in manuscript.

Place	Date	Hour	Summary of Events and Information	Remarks and references to Appendices
In the field	1/11/16		Company in the line in RAILWAY WOOD and POTIJZE SECTOR. Indirect fire during night. Enemy quiet.	
	2/11/16		Enemy quiet. Indirect fire at intervals throughout 24 hours on enemy communications. Enemy artillery active.	
	3/11/16		YPRES shelled. Indirect fire on enemy communications. Enemy artillery active between the hours of 9 am - 12 noon. British observation balloon broke loose and floated over to German lines in SOUTH EASTERLY direction. Indirect fire on enemy communication trenches and roads.	
	5/11/16		Raid on enemy trenches by BRIGADE on our LEFT. Two of our guns fired from dusk till dawn at enemy wire opposite RAILWAY WOOD. Indirect fire on enemy communications and OUTPOST buildings.	
	6/11/16		3 Guns in action during the night assisting BRIGADE on night RIGHT in making a raid on enemy trenches. Indirect fire throughout the day + night. RAILWAY WOOD heavily shelled during the day. Hostile French mortars landed in RAILWAY WOOD between the hours of 11 am & 1 pm.	
	7/11/16	p.m.	Relieved in sector by 164 M.G. Coy. Company moved to huts at BRANDHOEK.	
	8/11/16 9/11/16 10/11/16		Training resting at BRANDHOEK.	
	17/11/16	p.m.	Moved forward to ECOLE, N.E of YPRES	
	18/11/16	a.m.	Relieved 164 M.G. Coy in POTIJZE & RAILWAY WOOD sector in the early morning. Indirect fire on Enemy trenches and outpost buildings.	
	19/11/16		Quiet day. Indirect fire on HOOGE ROAD ROULERS RAILWAY and communication trenches.	
	20/11/16		Enemy quiet. Indirect fire on communication trenches.	
	21/11/16		Enemy machine guns active throughout the day in the sector. Indirect fire on BILL COTTAGE and enemy communication trenches.	
	22/11/16		Bombing activity in sags in front of RAILWAY WOOD. Enemy machine guns active in RAILWAY WOOD subsector. Indirect fire on communication trenches & BILL COTTAGE	
	23/11/16		German field guns active on our left sub-sector. Indirect fire on BILL COTTAGE ROULERS RAILWAY and communication trenches	

WAR DIARY or INTELLIGENCE SUMMARY

Army Form C. 2118

(Erase heading not required.)

Place	Date	Hour	Summary of Events and Information	Remarks and references to Appendices
In the field	24/11/16	a.m.	Enemy machine guns active throughout night against our aeroplanes. Indirect fire on communication trenches, RUPPRECHT FARM and roads	
	25/11/16		Situation normal. Enemy quiet.	
	26/11/16		Enemy quiet. Indirect fire on RUPPRECHT FARM & communication trenches	
	27/11/16		Enemy anti-aircraft guns active against our planes throughout the sector. Indirect fire on communication trenches behind enemy lines	
	28/11/16		Enemy field & heavy guns active at intervals throughout the day.	
	29/11/16	p.m. 4.50	Indirect fire on French Railways roads. Very misty. Two batteries of 6"R. raided enemy trenches. Indirect fire on enemy communication trenches	
	30/11/16		Enemy quiet. Indirect fire throughout day and night.	

Andrew Hand
Lieut for
O.C. 165th M.G. Coy.

Vol/2

War Diary
of the
165th M.G. Coy

for the period

1/1/17 to 31/1/17.

Army Form C. 2118

WAR DIARY or INTELLIGENCE SUMMARY

(Erase heading not required.)

165th M/G. Coy.

Place	Date	Hour	Summary of Events and Information	Remarks and references to Appendices
YPRES SALIENT	1-1-17		Artillery quiet. Trouble experienced with tunnel dug out at I.11.3. due to water. Night and day shifts at the pump found necessary. Operation Order No 3 (attached as Appendix A) amended as marked for Operation to be carried out tonight. The Artillery bombardment for this Operation opened at 5.50 p.m and stopped at 6.10 p.m.	App A ZERO 5.30 p.m
	2-1-17		Two emplacements at C.2.d.21 given up in RAILWAY WOOD. Dug out for I.11.3, tunneling employment, still uninhabitable through water. Work continued in order to render same inhabitable. Indirect fire carried out on enemy's support lines where observed by artillery during operation of last night, in order to prevent repair of same.	
	3-1-17		I.11.3. still water logged. Indirect fire as above for yesterday.	
	4-1-17		Normal trench routine.	
	5-1-17		Unusual enemy aircraft activity observed. One machine flew low over RAILWAY WOOD & was suspected of taking photographs to record instead condition of trenches. Indirect fire as per programme.	
	6-1-17	p.m	"B" Company relieved by 164 M.G. Coy. One section remained in RAMPARTS, remainder proceeded to A/Bde. Reserve Camp at BRANDHOEK.	
	7-1-17		Training at BRANDHOEK.	
	11-1-17	p.m	2nd Company relief of Section in RAMPARTS YPRES.	
	12-1-17		Training at BRANDHOEK.	
	13-1-17	9am	One Section & a half of the Company (6 guns) proceeded on detachment duty with appointment transport to ABEELE. Detachment is for anti-aircraft duty & under orders of O.C. "B" Battery. Three men detailed for searchlight work. This detachment relieved a similar detachment of 114 M.G. Coy. Daily training is also carried out so far as possible in circumstances.	BEF. Stor 27 NW L36 4.1.
	3pm	Company less above detachment of Section in RAMPARTS proceeded with CORPS RESERVE AREA - via to K Camp - for training purposes.	
	14-1-17		ANTI-AIRCRAFT DETACHMENT at ABEELE fire stunt guns arranged in three pairs, the stunt groups having fixed elevations of 20, 30 & 40 degrees.	

Army Form C. 2118

WAR DIARY
or
INTELLIGENCE SUMMARY

(Erase heading not required.)

165th M/G. Coy.

Instructions regarding War Diaries and Intelligence Summaries are contained in F.S. Regs., Part II. and the Staff Manual respectively. Title Pages will be prepared in manuscript.

Place	Date	Hour	Summary of Events and Information	Remarks and references to Appendices
YPRES SALIENT VIII Corps Reserve Area.	14-1-17 / 18-1-17	—	Training at "K" Camp. Training with limbers & pack mules greatly hampered by the fact that Transport lines remain at BRANDHOEK some distance from "K" Camp. Fifty limbers kept with Company & fully loaded.	
	15-1-17	—	Section of Company at RAMPARTS YPRES relieved by a section of 117 M.G. Coy. & regiment remainder of Coy.	
	19-1-17 / 20-1-17	—	Continuation of training at "K" Camp.	
	21-1-17	—	Company moved from "K" Camp to "Y" Camp (L.2.9.2.9.)	B.T.F. Sheet 27 N.W.
	22-1-17 / 31-1-17	—	Training continued at "Y" Camp	
	27-1-17	—	165th Inf. Bde. Operation Order No. 59 issued. This deals with movements of Troops & Corps Reserve in the event of a hostile attack taking place on VIII Corps front or on front of Corps on right & left. So far as it affects this Company, on receipt of mini "DEFENCE SCHEME MOVE TABLE A", we move at ZERO + 3 hours from our present camp "Y" to "K" Camp which is about a mile W. of us on the WATOU–POPERINGHE ROAD. On receipt of mini "DEFENCE SCHEME MOVE TABLE B" we move back at ZERO + 3 hours trek to our old divisional reserve camp at BRANDHOEK (H.7.a.1.4). On receipt of mini "DEFENCE SCHEME PREPARE" blankets, officers baggage etc. are to be stacked in our present camp & left in charge of 1 NCO & 1 man. This Company is ordered to make its own transport arrangements for above & other transport in accordance with above scheme have already been informed to lay transport after DETACHMENT at ABEELE according to about 00.89 will await special orders	B.T.F. Sheet 28 N.W.
	27-1-17		Training at "Y" Camp	
	31-1-17 / 31-1-17	—	Relief with the 65th Detachment at ABEELE	

J Newcroft.
O.C. 165th M.G.Coy.

SECRET

APPENDIX A

165TH M G Coy. OPERATION ORDERS No 3

Ref. Map ZILLEBEKE 1/10000
St JULIEN 1/10000

1. On the night ~~31st Dec/1st Jan~~ 1st/2nd Jany. there will be a bombardment by Artillery and Trench Mortars of the enemy front line, support line and communication trenches between I.6.c.15.05 – I.6.c.99.60 and I.6.a.08.90 – I.5.b.40.95, including front line, IBEX support, and IBEX reserve.

  The bombardment will last from ZERO to ZERO plus TWENTY MINUTES.

2. With the exception of Machine guns, Lewis guns, and a few infantrymen (who will fire very lights), the front line will be cleared from left of Brigade boundary to No 4 CRATER, including CAMBRIDGE TR, OAT TR and WOOD TRENCH at an hour before ZERO, and will return at the discretion of Bn Commanders at any time after ZERO plus ONE HOUR & TWENTY MINS.

3. During the remainder of the night machine guns will be active at regular intervals.

4. DISPOSAL OF MACHINE GUNS.

	GUN POSITION	TARGET	GUN TO BE MOVED
No 1 SECTION	I.4.d.15.15	TRAVERSE I.6.a.08.90 to I.6.c.40.40	X 2
	~~I.5.d.40.0~~ See amendment below	~~VERTICLE SEARCH~~ I.5.b.50.38 to I.5.b.40.95 SWINGING TRAVERSE to I.6.d.00.60 ~~AT MINIMUM ELEVATION~~	GULLY FARM ~~I.5.d.~~

-2-

	GUN FM	TARGET	GUN TO BE MOVED.
No 3 SECTION	~~I.10.d.90.70.~~	~~TRAVERSE~~ ~~I.6.c.30.75~~ ~~to~~ ~~I.6.c.60.55~~	~~RAILWAY FARM~~ ~~S.B.~~
	I.10.6.05.55.	TRAVERSE I.6.a.40.55 to I.6.a.70.43 SEARCH TO I.6.c.40.55	I.11.7.

5. ZERO HOUR will be notified later.

6. ACKNOWLEDGE.

Amendment to fire programme

| No 1 SECTION | I.11.c.88.56 | TRAVERSE FROM I.5b.40.95 to I.6.a.20.20 | H.21 |

COPIES.

O.C. No.1 SECTION
 "   " 2   "
 "   " 3   "
 "   " 4   "
File

30-12-16.

OFFICER COMMANDING
165 Machine Gun Coy.

CONFIDENTIAL.

VM 13

War Diary.
of
165th M. G. Coy.
for the period
1st to 28th February 1917.

WAR DIARY
or
INTELLIGENCE SUMMARY
(Erase heading not required.)

Army Form C. 2118

Place	Date	Hour	Summary of Events and Information	Remarks and references to Appendices
	1/18th		In Corps Reserve at V Camp. L 20, 2, 9. 2½ sections Divisional training	
	"		At Steele Park aircraft-station. 1½ sections	
	18th		Relieved 117th M.G.Coy in Potijze Railwood Sector. Everything very quiet.	
	19.		Enemy artillery active at intervals throughout the day on Ypres - Hell Fire corner, and Potijze road	
	20.		Enemy artillery fairly active. Indirect fire on enemy's C.T and Roads	
	21.		Very foggy all day. Good day for French repairs &c. Indirect fire Enemy artillery	
	22		became active about 7 p.m. Shelling near Potsam and Stones Dumps.	
			Foggy. Enemy M.G.s active at intervals during the night on left subsector	
	23.		Support line and roads	
	24.		Indirect fire on enemy C.Ts & Dumps. Otherwise situation quiet. Nothing unusual happened. Usual trench routine. Indirect Fire	
	25.		Mine exploded by enemy at 5.15 am N.E. of Railway Wood. Little damage was done. Enemy artillery active during the night against Ypres and Roads leading to Railway Wood	
	26.		Quiet day. During afternoon enemy fired about 20 T.M Bombs into Railway Wood	
			Our Artillery silenced them. Indirect fire	
	27.		The enemy howitzer registration about 10 a.m. Took over new Corps scheme emplacements I 10.1 and I 10.4. Quiet day. Coy took over new positions I 4.1	
	28.		Brigade extended its line to the left. Coy took over new positions. Indirect fire.	
			I 5.1 and I 5.2. Quiet day	

Andrew Kerr
M/C 165 M.G. Coy.

Vol 14

War Diary
of the
165th M. G. Coy
for the period
1st to 31st March
1917

WAR DIARY
or
INTELLIGENCE SUMMARY

(Erase heading not required.)

Army Form C. 2118

Instructions regarding War Diaries and Intelligence Summaries are contained in F.S. Regs., Part II. and the Staff Manual respectively. Title Pages will be prepared in manuscript.

Place	Date	Hour	Summary of Events and Information	Remarks and references to Appendices
Railway Wood Sector, YPRES	1/3/17		Coy in trenches. Indirect fire on enemy communications and dumps. Quiet day. Cooperated with artillery in supporting fighting patrols which went out inflicts at various times throughout the night.	
	2		Enemy shelled Ypres.	
	3		YPRES shelled intermittently throughout the day – Quiet in trenches – Indirect fire	
	4		Nothing to report.	
	5		Enemy shelled YPRES during night. Enemy Indirect machine guns more active than usual.	
	6		Coy relieved by 166 M.G.Coy. – Coy proceeded to billets in Brandhoek.	
	7		No 1 and 3 sections relieved two sections of 196 M.G.Coy in the L bis ELVERDINGHE	
	7/12		No 1 and 3 sections at ELVERDINGHE. Nothing to report.	
			No 2 and 4 sections training.	
	12		No 1 and 3 sections were relieved by 2 and 4 sections in L bis ELVERDINGHE	
	13		No 1 and 3 sections carried out Brigade sports	
	13/16		Training. No 1 & 3 sections. No 2 and 4 sections at ELVERDINGHE	
	16		Relieved 166 M.G.Coy in Railway Wood Sector.	
	17		Aeroplane activity on both sides – German plane brought down –	
	18		Aeroplane activity otherwise quiet –	
	19		Our artillery active against enemy positions and OP's at intervals throughout the day.	
	20		Quiet day – weather bad.	
	21		Hostile artillery active against YPRES and Railway Wood otherwise quiet.	
	22		Indirect fire as usual and firing salvos of 18 pdrs. HELLFIRE CORNER & MUD LANE shelled. Three enemy observation balloons up during day.	
	23		Enemy shelled front line. French mortar activity on both sides between 4 p.m. & 6 p.m. Enemy machine guns quieter than usual.	

1875 Wt. W593/826 1,000,000 4/15 J.B.C. & A. A.D.S.S./Forms/C. 2118.

WAR DIARY
or
INTELLIGENCE SUMMARY

(Erase heading not required.)

Army Form C. 2118

Place	Date	Hour	Summary of Events and Information	Remarks and references to Appendices
RAILWAY WOOD SECTOR	23rd March		Enemy aeroplanes active.	
	24th		Indirect fire as usual. M.guns cooperate with artillery at intervals during night on enemy transport approaches. Indirect fire as usual. British Armies in France adopt Summertime. All clocks at 11 pm being put forward one hour. Strong co-operation with artillery cancelled between 7.30 pm & 2 pm. Our aeroplanes active. Enemy artillery active.	
	25th		Enemy artillery very active between 7.30 pm & 8.30 pm. Enemy aeroplane brought down near ZILLEBEKE up during day. Enemy aeroplane flew at a very low altitude along Brigade front. Four enemy balloons	
		5.50 pm	Enemy exploded mine at junction of MUD LANE & firing line. Both sides bombarded heavily.	
			Weather bright & clear	
	26th	12.45 am	Enemy raided front line S. of MENIN ROAD. Brigade Left Battalion sent a raiding party out about 3am. Enemy machine guns active during early part of morning.	
			Weather cold & wet.	
	27th		During afternoon our artillery shelled new crater. Enemy shelled YPRES & HELL FIRE CORNER at about 8pm.	
	28th		Enemy shelled YPRES during afternoon & evening. L/CPL J.R.JENKINS killed.	
	29th		Very quiet day. Weather dull & wet.	
	30th		Enemy artillery active. Good day for observation.	
	31st		Artillery active on both sides. Our aeroplanes active.	

M.Mason Lt.
Act O.C. 165 MACHINE GUN COY

Vol 15

War Diary.
of
165th M.G. Coy
for the period
1st April to 30th April, 1917.

Confidential.

Army Form C. 2118

WAR DIARY
or
INTELLIGENCE SUMMARY
(Erase heading not required.)

Instructions regarding War Diaries and Intelligence Summaries are contained in F. S. Regs., Part II. and the Staff Manual respectively. Title Pages will be prepared in manuscript.

Place	Date	Hour	Summary of Events and Information	Remarks and references to Appendices
YPRES SALIENT.	1/4/17		Activity normal. Machine guns co-operation with artillery in connexion with a raid by 9th K.L Regt firing on enemy communications as per O.O.15 attached hereto as Appendix Z. No unusual circumstances attended this operation.	Appendix Z
	2/4/17		Activity normal -	BELGIUM Sheet 28.NW 1/20.000
	3/4/17		" "	
	4/4/17		" "	
	5/4/17		" "	
	6/4/17		Company relieved by 166 M.G. Coy. Relief normal & unattempted by enemy. After relief Company marched to a new camp consisting of huts in neighborhood of "C" Camp. G.6.a.4.7.	
	7/4/17			
	8/4/17			
	9/4/17		Improvement of new Camp	
	10/4/17		Trainings	
	11/4/17			
	12/4/17			
	13/4/17			
	14/4/17			
	15/4/17			
	16/4/17			
	16/4/17	4 p.m.	3 teams left camp with equipment on pack mules to relieve three teams of 166 M.G Coy in the line. This relief was completed by 7.30 p.m., the use of pack mules for effecting relief in daylight seems to be very useful.	
	"	9 p.m.	Remainder of Coy left camp to relieve remainder of 166 M.G. Coy in the line. Relief effected by 12.30 midnight.	
	17/4/17		Activity normal.	
	18/4/17		" "	
	19/4/17		Activity normal.	

R. Rawson Lt.

Army Form C. 2118

Instructions regarding War Diaries and Intelligence Summaries are contained in F.S. Regs., Part II. and the Staff Manual respectively. Title Pages will be prepared in manuscript.

WAR DIARY
or
INTELLIGENCE SUMMARY
(Erase heading not required.)

Place	Date	Hour	Summary of Events and Information	Remarks and references to Appendices
YPRES SALIENT	20/4/17			
	21/4/17		Activity in line normal. Considerable aircraft activity by both sides. Our antiaircraft M/guns seem effective.	
	22/4/17			
	23/4/17			
	24/4/17		Enemy machine gun activity below normal	
	25/4/17			
	26/4/17			
	27/4/17			
	28/4/17			
	29/4/17			
	29/4/17	11 pm	Enemy batteries commenced shelling ECOLE, in vicinity of M.G.Coy. H.Qrs, used 5.9" shells, about 3 pm arrived	
	30/4/17	2.30	Enemy shelling as above ceased. It is certain that our H.Qrs were not deliberately shelled and fortunately the buildings were only on the outer fringe of the enemy barrage. The target aimed at by the enemy was the position of the ECOLE containing two guns of 33rd Divn which had been firing occasionally on S.O.S. signals from this front. They had been firing on the evening of the 29th & probably their position had been spotted by the enemy in consequence, as they had not previously registered by the enemy artillery. Our H.Qrs building only received one hit which smashed a trestle, water tank & latrine, but considerable damage was done to the road by which our ration limbers arrive. Numerous large craters were made in the road which will take some time to repair. It was fortunate that our ration limbers convoy had just gone when the shelling commenced. Normal activity in the line	

E.Ramus Lt.
for O.C. 165th M.G.Coy.

"WAR DIARY"   Appendix Z.

165TH MACHINE GUN COMPANY   COPY No 5

OPERATION ORDER No. 15.

REF. TRENCH MAP ZILLEBEKE 1/10,000 & ST. JULIEN   1st APRIL 1917

1. The 9th KINGS will carry out an operation tonight against the enemy post about I.11.d.88.48 on S.W. edge of CRATER 5 as located by various patrols during the last few nights.

2. COMPOSITION OF PARTY
   a. Fighting Patrol. 1 Officer, 1 N.C.O. and 6 men.
   b. Covering party. 1 Officer, 1 N.C.O., 1 Lewis gun with 3 gunners, 6 riflemen.

   [...] Nursing Cheddar brains at [...] consists of R. Sutherin

3. ROUTE OF DEPARTURE AND RETURN.
   a. Fighting Patrol. Junction of Bays in trench I.11.d and I.11.b.
   b. Covering party. Just South of the CRATER

4. MACHINE GUNS. Five guns of this Company will co-operate as follows, fire being opened with the Field Artillery at ZERO minus 2 and being maintained until ZERO plus 30. Fire will also be continued in bursts through the remainder of the night on the same targets.

   (a) The X.2 gun will fire under orders from LT. NAIRN so as to enfilade IBEX AVENUE and DRIVE from I.6.a.7.7 to C.30.d.65.00.

   (b) The I.11.1 gun will fire under orders from 2 LT SCOUTS so as to enfilade ICE AVENUE from I.6.c.4.5 to I.6.c.95.65.

   (c) The I.11.2 gun will fire under orders from 2LT. BLACK so as to enfilade IDEA AVENUE from I.6.c.5.2 to I.6.d.8.9.

   (d) The I.10.1 gun will fire under orders from LT. HANSEN so as to search area I.12.a.80.65 – I.12.b.05.05 – I.12.b.32.05 – I.12.b.20.85.

   (e) The I.10.2 gun, also under orders from LT. HANSEN will fire so as to enfilade IDIOT ROW from I.12.b.32.5 to I.7.a.2.6.

- 2 -

5. ZERO HOUR.   10 pm.

6. SYNCHRONIZATION   LT. NAIRN & 2LT. COUTTS will synchronise at LEFT Battalion HQs. Synchronized time will be sent from Company HQs to LT. HANSEN and 2 LT. BLACK.

COPY   1 - LT. NAIRN
  "   2 - 2/LT. BLACK
  "   3 - 2/LT COUTTS
  "   4 - LT. HANSEN
       5 - Spare
       6 - File

                              O C. 165 M. G C°y

Vol 16

War Diary
of
165th M.G. Coy.
for the period
May 1st to 31st - 1917

CONFIDENTIAL

WAR DIARY or INTELLIGENCE SUMMARY

(Erase heading not required.)

Army Form C. 2118

165th M/G. Coy.

Place	Date	Hour	Summary of Events and Information	Remarks and references to Appendices
YPRES SALIENT [RAILWAY WOOD SECTOR]	1/5/17 to 6/5/17		Situation Normal. Little enemy artillery activity on forward area. Most of his artillery activity confined to back areas – particularly in and around YPRES. Weather very favourable. Considerable aerial activity. Machine guns very active against enemy aircraft.	
"	7/5/17	11 a.m.	Our Field Artillery practised a creeping barrage on enemy front. Machine guns (8) were originally to have co-operated with indirect fire on enemy approaches, but this arrangement was cancelled. Barrage appeared to be very effective although there were several gaps in it, which machine gun barrage fire could probably have covered.	
"	7/5/17 to 11/5/17		Activity Normal. Artillery & aerial activity in proportion to weather conditions. Weather very fine, but varied from time to time from point of view of observation. Machine guns very active against enemy aircraft – apparently with very good results.	
"	night 11/12 May	11 p.m.	Machine guns of this Company co-operated very successfully in a raid carried out by 1/9th Kings Liverpool Regt. on OSKAR FARM and trenches in vicinity. Eight guns were employed, firing on selected targets, principally communications. The raid proved very successful – six live prisoners being captured.	See App. Y O.O. 21.
"	12/5/17	–	During enemy shelling of forward area a 5.9" shell dropped on roof of staircase of main dug out under MENIN ROAD at our M.G. position I 17.1. Staircase was broken in and fumes of shell penetrated down into the dug-out. The gun team suffered badly from the fumes until they put their Gas Box Respirators on. These had been recently fitted with the new extension, and were proved to be quite effective against the fumes.	

Army Form C. 2118

1866
M/G. Coy.

WAR DIARY
or
INTELLIGENCE SUMMARY
(Erase heading not required.)

Instructions regarding War Diaries and Intelligence Summaries are contained in F. S. Regs., Part II. and the Staff Manual respectively. Title Pages will be prepared in manuscript.

Place	Date	Hour	Summary of Events and Information	Remarks and references to Appendices
YPRES SALIENT [RLY WOOD SECTOR]	12/5/17 to 16/5/17		Activity normal in conformity with fine weather. Considerable aircraft activity by both sides. Machine Guns very active against enemy aircraft with apparently good results. Heavy enemy artillery activity against back area.	
"	Night 16/17 May		Relief of Company in trenches by 166th Machine Gun Company in accordance with Brigade orders & Company Operation Order No. 22. attached in Appendix X. Relief completed from 11.30 p.m. to 3 a.m. approximately. Company when relieved proceeded to Billets in POPERINGHE by Route March.	See App X for O.O. 22.
POPERINGHE	17/5/17	-	Nothing to record beyond preparations of train movement to training area. to dispatch by 11.20 a.m. train of billets. P=5 - LT. STETCH and 2.O.R. = 1/G BOLLEZEELE. Company less mounted portion entrained at POPERINGHE STATION to proceed to WATTEN.	"
"	18/5/17	11.am		"
"	18/5/17	2 pm	Mounted portion of Company proceeded by road for BOLLEZEELE	"
WATTEN BOLLEZEELE	18/5/17	5 pm	Company detrained at WATTEN STATION and proceeded by ROUTE MARCH to BOLLEZEELE arriving there at about 7.30 p.m. and being accommodated in Billets.	"
HERZEELE	Night 18/19 May	-	Mounted portion of Company billeted for night at HERZEELE.	"
BOLLEZEELE	19/5/17		Mounted portion of Company arrived at BOLLEZEELE at about mid-day.	"
"	20/5/17 to 31/5/17		Training in and around BOLLEZEELE. Particular attention being paid to training for Open Warfare, and to getting the men fit, after the period of 30 days just completed in the trenches. Great attention also paid to practice of Machine Gun Barrage Drill.	"

E.P.Owens Lt
for O.C. 165th Machine Gun Coy.

1875 Wt. W593/826 1,000,000 4/15 J.B.C. & A. A.D.S.S./Forms/C. 2118.

SECRET. 165TH MACHINE GUN COMPANY   Appendix X
OPERATION ORDER No. 22.   COPY No. 7

REF:) TRENCH MAP. BELGIUM SHEET 28 N.W. 1/20000   16th May 1917
MAPS)   HAZEBROUCK   1/100000.

1. The 165th Machine Gun Company will be relieved in the line by the 166th Machine Gun Company on the night 16th/17th May.

2. GUIDES. Will probably not be required. If required arrangements will be notified later. O.C's Nos 1 & 4 Section will, however, arrange to guide the relieving Officer of No 4 Section from WEST LANE to No 4 Section's H.Q's.

3. HANDING OVER.

(a) All trench stores and belt boxes will be handed over and receipts taken. The receipts will be handed in to Orderly Room by 12 noon on the 17th inst.

(b) The receipts must show, in addition to the usual trench stores, all furniture, such as beds, tables, latrine boxes, etc, the Range Boards, Sentry Order Boards, and other emplacement boards. Separate receipts to be obtained for belt boxes. The 4 belt boxes of the CAMBRIDGE TR. Anti-aircraft team will be left at the I.11.1 position and will be handed over by that team for the A.A position.

(c) Fire programmes will be handed over to the relieving Officer, together with records of firing from 6am this morning. Indirect Fire guns will be relieved at their Indirect Fire positions, and suitable arrangements made to enable the Fire programme to be continued without interruption by the relief.

(d) Section Officers will personally show relieving Officers round their Sectors, and will hand over Section Cook houses for use, or retention until this Company is again in the line.

(e) All work in progress and contemplated will be handed over in writing.

4. All camp kettles, primus stoves, and tea cans will be returned to Coy Hqrs as early as possible this evening. To assist in this 2 men will be sent from the ECOLE to report to each Section Hqrs at 6.30 pm.

5. TRANSPORT. Will be required as follows:-
(a) Coy Hqrs. G.S. limber & Mess cart at Coy Hqrs
(b) No 1 section. G.S. limber at MENIN Rd R.E. dump
(c) No 2   "   "   "   YPRES RATION Dump POINT
(d) No 3   "   "   "   MENIN Rd R.E. dump
(e) No 4   "   "   "

The above Transport will be in position as soon as possible in conformity with traffic regulations - probably about 4.30 - 4.45 pm.

Officers chargers will be sent for Nos 1, 2 & 4 sections and for Coy Hqrs.

6. The CAMBRIDGE TR. A.H. team will hand their 4 belt boxes over to the I.H.I team at the end of evening "STAND TO", and will then report with their gun equipment and full kit to O.C. No 4 section in BEEK TR. for further orders.

7. The gun team of No 1 section at present at the ECOLE will, when relieved, load their gun equipment on No 1 section's limber at MENIN dump, and await the arrival of their section, when they will come under the orders of O.C. No 1 section.

8. REPORTS. Completion of relief will be notified to Coy Hqrs by each O.C. Section as soon as possible. The runners used for this purpose will proceed to billets with Hqrs party.

9. RETURN TO BILLETS.
(a) TRANSPORT. All transport will return direct to Transport lines, with the exception of the Mess cart and 1 Hqrs limber, which will proceed to Company billets in POPERINGHE to unload before returning to transport lines.

(2) Sections will proceed independently by Route March to billets in Brigade School, POPERINGHE.

10. 2/Lt. Brown has been detailed to take over the above billets at Brigade School this morning, and he will be responsible for providing each party with its billets on arrival.

11. BILLETING PARTY — Lt. STRETCH with his servant and one full corporal, will proceed by train from POPERINGHE at 11.19 am on the 17th inst to WATTEN whence they will proceed to BOLLEZEELE, and meet the Staff Captain at "THE SQUARE" at 9.30 am on the 18th inst to arrange the Coy. billets.

12. The Company (less mounted portion) will proceed by train from POPERINGHE at 11.19 am on the 18th inst, will detrain at 3pm WATTEN, and will thence march to BOLLEZEELE. They will be met just outside BOLLEZEELE by the billeting party, & conducted to the Company billets.

13. The Transport will move to BOLLEZEELE with 7th King's and 165 Bde. H.Q. Transport, by Route march, under the orders of the Brigade Transport Officer. Starting time 2pm on the 18th inst.

COPY No 1 — O.C. No 1 Section
" 2 " " 2 "
" 3 " " 3 "
" 4 " " 4 "
" 5 " TRANSPORT
" 6 FILE
" 7 WAR DIARY
" 8 STAFF

C. Parrott
for
O.C. 165 MACHINE GUN Coy.

APPENDIX Y

165TH MACHINE GUN COMPANY
OPERATION ORDER No 21   COPY No 6

REF TRENCH MAPS, ZILLEBEKE &   10th May 1917
    ST. JULIEN 1/10000

1. On the night 11th/12th May a party composed of 2 Officers and 40 men of the 9th Kings Liverpool Regt. will carry out a raid on the enemy's front trenches from, and including, the Sap at I.6.c.05.82 to I.6.c.00.95.

2. STARTING POINT - Our front line between I.5.d.46.57 and I.5.d.41.66.

3. MACHINE GUNS - Five guns of this Company will cooperate with Indirect Fire on the following targets, in accordance with the attached programme :-

    I.   THE STABLES (I.5.b.7.6.)
    II. IBEX DRIVE and IBEX AVENUE
    III. C.T. running between I.6.c.9.9 and J.1.a.3.6
    IV. THE RAILWAY
    V.   WILDE WOOD

4. TIME and DURATION OF FIRE - Fire will be opened at ZERO and cease at ZERO + 20.

5. ZERO HOUR - will be notified later.

6. SYNCHRONIZATION - Synchronised time will be sent from Coy. HQrs. to O.C. No.1 section, & O.C. No.3 section; O.C. No.2 section will obtain synchronised time from Left Battalion HQrs.

COPY No 1 - O.C. No 1 section
  " No 2 - O.C. " 2 "
     No 3 - O.C. " 3 "
     No 4 - O.C. " 4 " (for information)
     No 5 - FILE
     No 6 - WAR DIARY
     No 7 - B SECT. 196 M.G.Coy.
     No 8 - 165 INF. BDE

C Parsons
for O.C. 165TH MACHINE GUN Coy

165th Machine Gun Company

OPERATION ORDER No 21.

FIRE PROGRAMME

OFFICER	GUN	GUN POSTN. (APPROX)	TARGET
2/Lt BLACK	CAMBRIDGE 1st AA.	Close to position below	THE STABLES Area I.5.b.65.40 – I.6.b.83.45 – I.5.b.70.71 – I.5.b.47.62
	I.4.2	I.4.c.80.39	I'BEK DRIVE I.6.a.46.75 – I.6.b.29.86
2/Lt BROWN	I.10.2.	I.10.b.02.03 OLD X LINE	C.T. I.6.c.92.82 – I.6.b.52.73
	ECOLE	–do–	–do– –do–
2/Lt. SMALLWOOD	I.11.2.	I.11.c.48.94	RAILWAY I.6.d.12.60 – I.6.b.70.90
Lt ESSON 196th M.G.Coy	RAMPARTS	OLD X LINE	I'BEK AVENUE I.6.a.47.47 – I.6.a.73.64
	–do–	–do–	–do– –do–
	–do–	I.12.d.6.9.	WILDE WOOD

Officers will select suitable gun positions at, or close to, the positions mentioned in the above table, and will forward exact map references of their guns positions to Coy. HQrs by 4 p.m. today.

11th May 1917

163rd Machine Gun Company

Appendix "A" to Operation Order No. 21

The following details of quadrant elevations and directions of fire have been calculated from the gun positions reported and should be used as a check on Section Officers' own calculations:-

OFFICERS	GUN	POSITION	TARGET	DIRECTION (MAP BEARING)	QUADRANT ELEVⁿ	RANGE YDS
Lt Black	CAMERONS 10 M.G.	I.u.d.28.58	THE STABLES	63° - 67.5°	3° 30"	1800
	I.M.G.	I.4.b.50.34	IBEX DRIVE	72°	5° 35"	2200
2Lt Brown	NORTH GUN	I.10.b.02.03	C.T.	65-0°	5° 10"	2150
	SOUTH GUN	I.10.d.05.92	C.T.	65°	6° 30"	2350
Lt Smallwood	I.M.G.	I.R.c.81.90	RAILWAY	55°	2° 45"	1600
Lt Eason	NORTH GUN	I.10.b.08.60	IBEX AVENUE	61.9°	4° 16"	2000
	SOUTH "	I.10.b.08.53	- " -	61.5°	3° 47"	1900
	WEST LANE GUN	I.10.d.63.89	WILDE WOOD	57.5° - 61.5°	6° 0"	2300

Guns firing on Communication trenches should have a traverse of 1° to right and 1° to left of their calculated direction of fire

11th May 1917.

CONFIDENTIAL

War Diary
of
165th M.G. Coy.
for the period
June 1st to June 30th, 1917

WAR DIARY
INTELLIGENCE SUMMARY.
(Erase heading not required.)

Army Form C. 2118.

Instructions regarding War Diaries and Intelligence Summaries are contained in F. S. Regs., Part II. and the Staff Manual respectively. Title pages will be prepared in manuscript.

Place	Date	Hour	Summary of Events and Information	Remarks and references to Appendices
BOLLEZEELE (FRANCE)	1st June	—	} Continuation of training. Several days spent in practising a trench to trench attack on trenches just East of RAILWAY WOOD YPRES. Previously arranged for 7 guns to advance with third wave of Infantry — further 6 left in 2nd position until 3rd objective was captured & then to proceed to their allotted positions. All these 13 guns two for left flank protection, & one for right flank protection and the remaining five for general defence of new front line. Ammunition supply was arranged for by grouping guns & allotting them to one of three forward dumps. Ammunition was to be carried from the dumps with 1st objective by a carrying party of 24 men (2 per gun) inclusive of four N.C.O.'s & three to each gun. The proposed [ ] attack was however cancelled & all training first suspended on 9.6.17.	
"	2nd "	—		
"	3rd "	—		
"	4th "	—		
"	5th "	—		
"	6th "	—		
"	7th "	—		
"	8th "	—		
"	9th "	—		
"	10th "	—		
YPRES SALIENT	11th June	—	The Company moved from BOLLEZEELE into the trenches East of YPRES relieving the 164th M.G. Coy.	See O.O. 23
"	"	—	The Sector so taken over was North of the Sector previously occupied by this Company and included 10 positions in the front trenches, 3 in YPRES DEFENCES (KRATIE SALIENT), & 3 in reserve on CANAL BANK at Coy H.Qrs. Relief the last six guns were brought up to trenches on pack mules across country in daylight.	See Map attached to O.O.
"	12th "	3.30 am	Relief completed at 3.30 a.m. Conducted without casualties.	
"	13th "		Normal trench routine all day. Shelling fairly severe all day.	

JMR

WAR DIARY
INTELLIGENCE SUMMARY

Army Form C. 2118.

Place	Date	Hour	Summary of Events and Information	Remarks and references to Appendices
YPRES SALIENT	12/6/17	10 p.m.	Enemy gas shell bombardment of YPRES, DEAD END & CANAL BANK. Company HQrs felt	
	13/6/17	3 a.m.	the full effects but wearing of box respirators proved perfectly satisfactory, no casualties resulted	
"	14/6/17	—	Normal routine. One casualty (slight)	
"	14/6/17	—	One casualty (slight) evacuated to Field Ambulance. Relieved at night previous by 166th M.G. Coy on our right. 70th our	See MAP Appendix P
			7 & other positions from 116th M.G. Coy on our left; Brigade frontage therefore moved NORTH includes WIELTJE. Locations WIELTJE. Four M. Guns are sited in Uhlans' (WIELTJE) different trenches; a tunnelled system connecting up all the emplacements.	
"	15/6/17	—	One casualty – died from wounds same day. Took over 20 other positions from 116th M.G. Coy and handed over four positions to 166th M.G. Coy.	
"	16/6/17	—	Nothing to report.	
"	17/6/17	—	Heavy shelling in vicinity of CANAL BANK (DEADEND). One Officer 2nd Lt T.N. SMALLWOOD dangerously wounded. Heavy gas shelling during evening in same vicinity in YPRES	
"	18/6/17	—	Normal routine. Heavy shelling - back areas	
"	19/6/17	—	Three positions taken over from 166th M.G. Coy. Front positions now extend on 2 Section of 190th Bgde attached to us attached Maps R [?]	Appendix P
"	20/6/17 – 22/6/17	—	Normal activity and heavy shelling particularly in back areas. One casualty on 20/6/17	
"	23/6/17	—	Operation Order No 24 issued for an Operation to take place on 24th/25th	0.0.24 circulated

A6945 Wt. W11422/M1160 350,000 12/16 D.D. & L. Forms/C./2118/14.

Army Form C. 2118.

WAR DIARY
or
INTELLIGENCE SUMMARY.
(Erase heading not required.)

Instructions regarding War Diaries and Intelligence Summaries are contained in F. S. Regs., Part II. and the Staff Manual respectively. Title pages will be prepared in manuscript.

Place	Date	Hour	Summary of Events and Information	Remarks and references to Appendices
YPRES SALIENT (NIEELJE)	24/6/17	—	Normal activity. Level bombardment of trench areas. Operation Order No 24 cancelled owing to cancellation of the proposed operation. Enemy plane brought down by fire from one of our machine guns	
"	25/6/17		Normal activity. Unusual hostile artillery activity against trench areas. One casualty	
"	26/6/17 – 28/6/17		" Rather less activity by enemy artillery	
"	29/6/17	6.15 p.m – 6.45 p.m	Practice Machine Gun Barrage carried out with group of 8 guns. Two barrages without change of direction but change of range from 1880 yds to 2200 yds, a third barrage with change of direction of 13° and change of range to 2000 yds. No hostile retaliation. So far as could be judged the Barrage Practice was carried out with success.	
"	30/6/17	—	Normal activity all day. Enemy artillery more active on front areas but not very active on back areas.	
"	30/6/17	—	Operation Order No 25 issued for a Raid to be attempted tonight. 5 machine guns to co-operate.	OO 25 attached
"	1/7/17	1.15 a.m	Raid attempted but spoilt by enemy coming out in front of his wire & bombing the raiding party. Machine guns fired successfully without casualties. One casualty from m.g bullet when preparing position for firing.	

J H Parsons Lt
for O.C. 165 M.G. Coy.

185TH MACHINE GUN COY
OPERATION ORDER No 24

FIRE PROGRAMME

OFFICER	GUN	GUN POSITION (APPROX)	TARGET
2nd Lt. STORGE C SECTION 196 M.G.Coy	C.27.4	CONGREVE WALK C.28.c.19.18	GRAVENSTAFEL ROAD from C.23.c.83.55 to C.23.d.20.85
	C.27.5	— do —	CAMBRAI AVENUE from C.23.d.1.3. to C.23.d.50.60
2nd Lt. BLACK No 2 SECTION and 2nd Lt. HALSTEAD	C.28.4	NEAR PAGODA ST about C.28.d.15.50	CAMBRAI DRIVE from C.23.d.00.48 to C.23.d.80.18
	C.28.5	— do —	PLUM FARM C.24.c.
	I.4.1	TROUSE TR about I.4.6.35.55	CAMEL TR from C.29.a.95.15 to C.29.a.98.35

Officers will select suitable gun positions at, or close to, the positions mentioned in the above table, and will forward exact map references of their gun positions to Coy. HQrs by mid-day tomorrow 24th June.

23rd June 1917

SECRET.   165TH MACHINE GUN COY
                OPERATION ORDER No 24   COPY No. 6

REF. TRENCH MAPS, ZILLEBEKE
              & ST JULIEN 1/10000   23rd June 1917

1.   On the night 24th/25th June a party of 6th K.L.R, composed of 1 Officer and 20 men, supported by two bombing squads of 4 men each, will carry out a raid on the enemy's front trench from C.29.a.48.63 to C.29.a.40.70 - length about 50 yards.

2.   STARTING POINT. - Our front line at about C.29.a.2.1

3.   MACHINE GUNS. - Five guns of this Company will co-operate with Indirect Fire on the following targets, in accordance with attached programme :-

                1.   CAMEL TRENCH
                2.   CAMBRAI DRIVE
                3.   PLUM FARM
                4.   GRAVENSTAFEL ROAD
                5.   CAMBRAI AVENUE

4.   TIME & DURATION OF FIRE.   Fire will be opened at ZERO, with the opening of Artillery Barrage, and will cease at ZERO + 20.

5.   ZERO HOUR -   will be notified later.

6.   SYNCHRONISED TIME.   Synchronised time will be sent from Company Headquarters to O.C. C. Section 196th M.G.Coy, and also to O.C. No. 2 section. Failing this synchronised time is to be obtained from Battalion HQrs. in POTIJZE WOOD.

COPY No.1 - O.C. C. SECTION 196 M.G.COY
    "   2 - O.C. No. 2 SECTION
    "   3 - O.C. " 4 " (for information).
    "   4 - 165TH INF. BDE
    "   5 - FILE   H Parsons Lt
    "   6 - WAR DIARY   for O.C
    "   7 - SPARE.
                                    165TH MACHINE GUN COY

Appendix P

B.K.V.
16.5.17

SECRET   165TH MACHINE GUN COY   COPY N° 4

OPERATION ORDER No. 23

REFERENCE MAPS.
TRENCH MAP ST. JULIEN & ZILLEBEKE
HAZEBROUCK
BELGIUM 28 N.W
2

10th June 1917

1. This Company will relieve 164th Machine Gun Coy in the Left Sector of the Divisional Front on the night 11th/12th June.

2. Dispositions of Sections in the line will, so far as is known at present, be as follows:-

   LEFT SECTOR — Positions - C.27.5. C.28.4. C.28.5. —
       3 Guns No. 1 section, Lt Hansen & 2Lt Cain.

   CENTRE SECTOR — Positions I.4.1. I.5.1. I.5.2 —
       3 Guns No 2 section, 2Lt Black, 2Lt Brown

   RIGHT SECTOR — Positions I.3.1, I.4.2, I.5.3.
       3 Guns No.3 section, Lt Bray, 2Lt Smallwood.

   RESERVE — No. 4 section and spare guns of Nos. 1, 2 & 3 sections.

       2Lt Halstead will for the present remain at Transport lines.

3. GUIDES. Arrangements about guides will be notified later.

4. TAKING OVER. The usual trench stores will be taken over; Indirect Fire Schemes taken over and arrangements made to continue fire without interruption in accordance with programme. List of stores taken over to be forwarded to Coy Hqrs. by 12 noon on the 12th inst. Belt boxes will be taken over unless notification to the contrary is received.

5. SPARE PARTS. All spare parts boxes, and spare barrels, with the exception of 1 per section, to be sent to the Artificer prior departure for trenches.

6. RUNNERS. One spare man per section will be taken into the trenches and after bringing Relief Complete Report to Coy Hqrs will be retained at Hqrs.

7. Completion of relief will be notified to Coy HQrs by above Runners as soon as possible after relief.
       Section Officers will arrange for this Runner to accompany the Runner of the Officer they relieve to H.Qrs.

8. TRANSPORT - Arrangements will be notified later.

9. The Company will entrain at ESQUELBECQ tomorrow 11th. inst. at 9.30 am ; On arrival at ~~Pop~~ POPERINGHE will march to B Camp, and at night will move up to the line.

COPY No. 1 - O.C. No. 1 SECTION
No. 2 " 2 "
No. 3 " 3 "
No. 4 " 4 "
No. 5 O.C. TRANSPORT
No. 6 FILE
No. 7 WAR DIARY
No. 8 SPARE

G. Parrott Lt.
for
O.C. 165 MACHINE GUN COY

SECRET   165TH MACHINE GUN Coy
OPERATION ORDER No 25.   COPY No. 6.

REF. TRENCH MAPS. ZILLEBEKE
& ST. JULIEN 1/10000.   30th June 17.

1. On the night 30th June/1st July a party of 6th K.L.R, composed of 1 Officer and 20 men, supported by two bombing squads of 8 men each, will carry out a raid on the enemy's front trench at from about C.29.a 45 65 — length about 50 yds

2. STARTING POINT.   Our front line at about C.29.a.2.1

3. MACHINE GUNS.   Five guns of this company will co-operate with Indirect Fire on the following targets, in accordance with attached programme :—

   1.   UHLAN FARM
   2.   CAMBRAI DRIVE
   3.   PLUM FARM
   4.   GRAVENSTAFEL ROAD
   5.   CAMBRAI AVENUE

4. TIME & DURATION OF FIRE   Fire will be opened at ZERO, with the opening of Artillery Barrage, and will cease at ZERO + 35

5. RATE OF FIRE.   250 rounds per 5 minutes

6. ZERO HOUR — will be notified later.

7. SYNCHRONISED TIME.   Synchronised time will be obtained from Battalion H.Qrs in POTIJZE WOOD.

COPY No. 1 - O.C. B. SECTION 196 M G Coy (for information)
   "   2 - OC. No. 2 SECTION
   "   3 - OC. No. 4   "
   "   4 - 165 INF BDE
   "   5 - FILE
   "   6 - WAR DIARY
   "   7 - SPARE.

                        H Parrott
                   for O.C. 165TH MACHINE GUN Coy

165th MACHINE GUN COY.

OPERATION ORDER No. 25

FIRE PROGRAMME

OFFICER	GUN	GUN POSITION (approx)	TARGET
2nd Lt. Brown No. 4 Section	C.27.4.	Congreve Walk C.28.c.19.18	Gravenstafel Road from C.23.c.83.55 to C.23.d.20.85
	C.27.5.	—do—	Cambrai Avenue from C.23.d.1.3 to C.23.d.50.60
2nd Lt. Black No. 2 Section and 2nd Lt. Halstead	C.28.4.	Near Pagoda St. about C.28.d.15.50	Cambrai Drive from C.23.d.00.48 to C.23.d.80.18
	C.28.5.	—do—	Plum Fm C.24.c.
	I.4.1	Prowse Tr about I.4.b.35.55	Uhlan Farm C.29.b.

Officers will select suitable gun positions at, or close to, the positions mentioned in the above table.

30th June 1917.

Vol 18

War Diary

of the

165th M. G. Co.

for the period

1st July to 31st July,

1917.

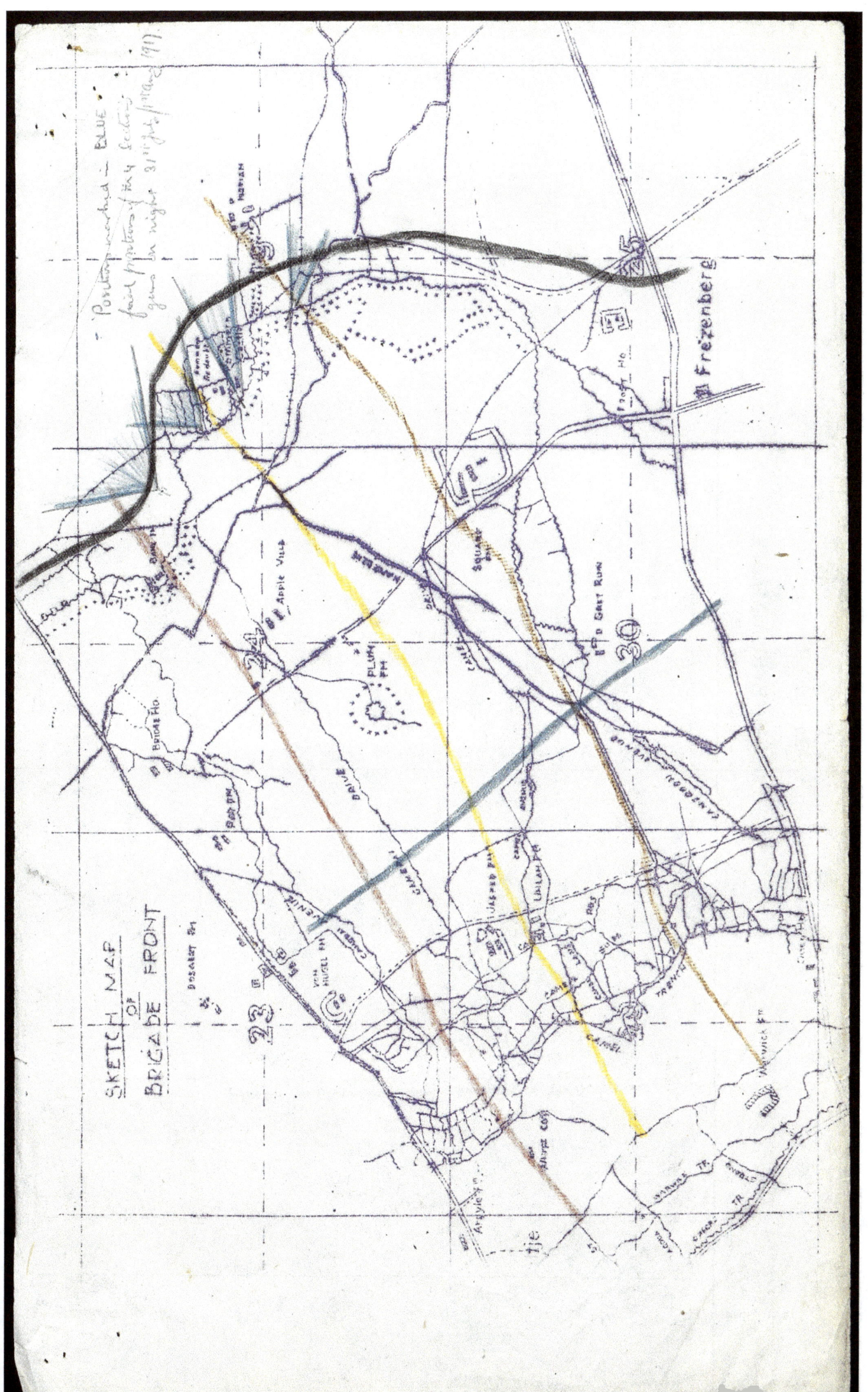

WARDIARY

INTELLIGENCE SUMMARY

(Erase heading not required.)

Army Form C. 2118

Instructions regarding War Diaries and Intelligence Summaries are contained in F.S. Regs., Part II. and the Staff Manual respectively. Title Pages will be prepared in manuscript.

Place	Date	Hour	Summary of Events and Information	Remarks and references to Appendices
YPRES SALIENT WELTJE SECTOR.	1/7/17.	—	Arrangements made for relief of Company by the 164th M.G. Coy on the night 2nd/3rd July. Company Operation Order No. 26 issued to Sections.	O.O. No 26 attached.
"	2/7/17	—	Operation Order No 27 issued to Sections concerned. 1 minute M.G. fire on certain selected targets in co-operation with artillery. Fire directed largely on No mans land, object to catch any enemy patrols, or any laying out parties who were in anticipation of a raid, ready to attack identification stunt from exploded or knocked enemy posts. Infantry warned of fire completed to them and identification. Relieved by 164th M.G. Coy. As much as possible relief carried out in daylight. Remainder by night.	O.O. No 27 B attached
"	3/7/17	12.30am	Relief complete. Company proceeded by Sections to RED ROSE CAMP. (BRANDHOEK)	
BRANDHOEK (RED ROSE CAMP)	3/7/17	4.20pm	Company (less mounted portion & Transport) at BRANDHOEK, and proceeded by train to LUMBRES (nr ST OMER). Mounted portion proceeded by ROUTE MARCH under Bde. Transport Officer starting at 2 a.m halting for night at WALLON CAPEL.	
—	3/7/17	7.30pm	Company (less mounted portion) arrived at LUMBRES & marched to billets at ZUTOVE in BOISDINGHEM AREA arriving at about 8.30pm.	
ZUTOVE	4/7/17	12 noon	Transport (horsed) arrived at BILLETS in good order. Remounts.	
"	5/7/17	—	Training under Coy arrangements.	
"	6/7/17	—	Training under Coy arrangements during morning	
—	6/7/17	2.30 pm	Company marched with Transport march to new billets at BAR BINGHEM in BOISANGHEM AREA.	

WAR DIARY
—or—
INTELLIGENCE SUMMARY

(Erase heading not required.)

Army Form C. 2118

Place	Date	Hour	Summary of Events and Information	Remarks and references to Appendices
BOTSDINGHEM AREA	7/9/17	—	Training on Area near Coy arrangements.	
	8/9/17 9/9/17 10/9/17 11/9/17 12/9/17 13/9/17 14/9/17 15/9/17 16/9/17 17/9/17 18/9/17 19/9/17 20/9/17	—	Training - Particular attention paid to Barrage Drill. Training schemes arranged by O.M.G.O. carried out. A good proportion of the time was spent practising the attack over a taped area corresponding to the German front just S.E. of WIELTJE. Two Sections Nos 1 & 4 were trained in attacking a Battalion No 1 Section detailed for 1st Objective (BLUE LINE). No 4 Section for 2nd Objective (BLACK LINE). Particular attention was paid to carrying up to ammunition supply each Section having 8 infantry men attached as ammunition carriers. Each team was allotted a definite portion to take up or make up objective line. Particular attention was also paid to communication & messages. Copies & Section Runners received special training under an Officer. Aeroplane photographs were very carefully studied & a model of the actual ground relief as shown by 1/10000 contoured map was made & carefully studied by all ranks.	
"	23/9/17	—	Two Sections Nos 1 & 4. Transport less Mess Cart & 3 chargers proceeded by Route March to forward area. Conforms operation order No. 27 & moved to position concerned.	OO.27 attached
—	24/9/17	—	Remainder portion of company, Mess Cart & 3 chargers proceeded by Route march to ST OMER & thence by train to forward area - part to ABEELE & part to POPERINGHE. Two sections Nos 1 & 4 then proceeded to BEDOUIN CAMP & remainder to RED ROSE CAMP. The latter proceeded to trenches at night.	

GMP

Army Form C. 2118

WAR DIARY
INTELLIGENCE SUMMARY
(Erase heading not required.)

Instructions regarding War Diaries and Intelligence Summaries are contained in F. S. Regs., Part II. and the Staff Manual respectively. Title Pages will be prepared in manuscript.

Place	Date	Hour	Summary of Events and Information	Remarks and references to Appendices
YPRES SALIENT. (between WIELTJE and POTIJZE WOOD)	21/7/17		Six M.G. positions taken up. Remaining two guns of No. 2 & 3 Sections remained at Company H.Qrs in POTIJZE WOOD.	
"	22/7/17 23/7/17 24/7/17		Usual Trench routine. In addition 6 guns were used for harassing fire under Divisional arrangements. Two guns fired by day and four by night according to a divisional fire programme issued from time to time. Targets were mainly trenches, approaches & dumps.	
	24/7/17	1 p.m.	6 guns were used for forming a M.G. Barrage covering a daylight raid made by 5th K.L.R. This raid proved quite successful.	
	25/7/17 to 30/7/17		Harassing fire by 6 guns continued. At the same time the positions detailed for No. 2 & 3 Sections forming "P" Battery in the forthcoming attack were reconnoitred and prepared for use. All necessary ammunition was also placed in position at selected dumps, & scattered in Steel Helmets near the Barrage positions. Company Operation Order No. 28 issued on the 26th July. Appendix A issued 28th-30th July.	OO 28 + Map attached. App A to OO 28 attached.
	29/7/17		Nos 1 & 4 Sections arrived in small parties at Coy H.Qrs POTIJZE WOOD after midday. "Q" Battery consisting of two Sections of 196th M.G. Coy also took up assembly positions at midday.	
	30/7/17		Y day. Shortly before dusk Nos 1 & 4 Sections proceeded to their assembly positions in support and Reserve trenches respectively. Nos 2 & 3 Sections proceeded to their assembly positions close to their first Barrage Positions & similarly "Q" Battery containing to two Sections of 196th Coy. The final work in preparation of Barrage positions was started after dusk	
	30/7/17		For M.G. Barrage Fire Organisation order see appendix 1A. This also includes the portions of directions & elevations worked out for the several Barrages.	Appendix 1A attached.

1875 Wt. W593/8266 1,000,000 4/15 J.B.C. & A. A.D.S.S./Forms/C. 2118.

WAR DIARY or INTELLIGENCE SUMMARY

Army Form C. 2118

Place	Date	Hour	Summary of Events and Information	Remarks and references to Appendices
YPRES SALIENT (WEILTJE – WARWICK FM Sector)	30/7/17	7.30 p.m.	C.O. moved up to Brigade Forward Command Post at MILL COTTS.	
	31/7/17		Z day. Intermittent shelling of our batty trenches all night, probably in retaliation for the gas shells fired during the night by our artillery.	
	"	3.50 a.m.	Zero hour. Our intense barrage opening up, enemy S.O.S. signal sent up & enemy artillery immediately increased its fire on the trenches in which it was already firing into. Apparently trenches (how supports were lying)	Diary of Bn H.Q.rs
	"	5.45 a.m.	First message received from N.C.O. i/c one of teams of No 1 Section (BLUE LINE) reporting his position & stating that he could not get in touch with other teams or other of his Section.	
	"	6.30 a.m.	P & Q batteries having finished firing at P.Q. position moved forward followed by pack mule ammunition column.	
	"	6.50 a.m.	Report received of casualties to Section officers of No 1 Section. Lt Hannan – reported seriously wounded.	
	"	7.45 a.m.	Message received from 9th Essex of Q Battery reporting O.C. Q Battery – Lt Whitby – killed, also reporting only one team of Q Battery arrived at Q.1 position.	
	"	10 a.m.	Message rec'd from N.C.O. i/c No 1 Section showing position of guns & reporting situation very favourable. Consolidating as fast as possible. Enemy artillery fairly active.	
	"	10 a.m.	Report received that Lt HANSEN O.C. No 1 Section died of wounds.	
	"	10.15 a.m.	2/Lt CAIN. O.C. "P" Battery. Pack Amm't Column called & reported pack mules drove up – lost two mules – obtained animals to be watered & fed & often used again for ammunition carrying	
			Found porch arrived & 166 M.G. Coy straggling – made them dump their ammunition at PLUM FARM. C.O.	BIP

WAR DIARY / INTELLIGENCE SUMMARY

Army Form C. 2118

Place	Date	Hour	Summary of Events and Information	Remarks and references to Appendices
YPRES SALIENT (WIELTJE-WARWICK FM SECTOR)	31/7/17	11.30am	Lt Sasse, O.C. Pack Animal Section Q Battery (194th Coy) reported personally that at time due for Q Battery to cease fire (Z+1h.23) he moved up to Q position & found that had Battery had had a considerable number of casualties (about 12 men). Battery moved up with mules after loading completed, by No 5 track as far as German front line, where they found two guns of Battery had lost direct. He took command & moved forward. Ground found to be bad for mules. He set mules loose & employed drivers to carry ammunition by hand arriving eventually at RAT FARM at 8.45am with 3 NCO's, 14 men, & 3 guns (without tripods). C.O. ordered Lt Sasse to return to Battery position & to link with the Battery Officer (Q Battery) (2nd Lt Esson) or P Battery, & to get all available guns laid on S.O.S lines, & to get ammunition for available guns up to at least 50,000 rounds.	Diary of Coy HQr
"	"	12.30pm	C.O. sent message to O.C. No1 Section in BLACK LINE to move forward to BLACK LINE to reinforce No 4 Section, leaving his guns in the BLUE LINE one on each flank. Action reported by message to O.C. No 4 Section.	
"	"	2.30pm	C.O. received message from 2 Lt Brown O.C. No 2 section (Barrage P Battery) reporting that he had reached P2 position but was unable to complete his programme of firing owing to heavy shell fire. He reported that he was then digging in close to Barrage position (12 men) under 4.2" shrapnel fire. Rest of casualties also reported 1 killed, 3 wounded the latter including Section Sgt. Similar message containing similar report received from O.C. P Battery - Lt Ramage - 3 reported casualties to No 3 Section, 3 wounded including Section Sgt.	
"	"	2.30pm	The C.O. sent message to Capt Faure O.C. 196th M.G. Coy reporting situation as regards "Q" Battery & informing him of action taken. (Sui orders to 2 Lt SASSE).	
"	"	6pm	C.O. sent message to O.C. No 1 Section (BLUE LINE) to cancel order to send two (two) guns to POMMERN REDOUBT & to keep them in position in flank of BLUE LINE	

WAR DIARY
INTELLIGENCE SUMMARY

Army Form C. 2118.

Place	Date	Hour	Summary of Events and Information	Remarks and references to Appendices
YPRES SALIENT (WIELTJE-WARWICK Fm SECTOR)	31/7/17	6.10pm	Situation of B Battery again reported by CO to OC 194th MG Coy. Reported as 4 guns approximately in or near Q1 posn, & 3 guns in BLUE LINE. Continued but being employed bunch of SAA being found in BLUE LINE. Estimated casualties to B Battery about 15 killed & wounded.	Diary of Coy HQrs
"	"	7.30pm	Order sent to 2/Lt HALSTEAD O/C HQr Section to collect every available MG 3 am to carry up belt boxes to BLUE LINE. Situation in front line serious owing to shortage of SAA and expected counter attack.	
"	"	7.30pm	Runner & message from OC No1 Section BLUE LINE (despatched 7.20pm) stating that OC No.4 Section (between BLUE LINE) could not be found & it was impossible to get through there. Also reporting 1 gun in each flank (of the BLUE LINE and 2 guns in BLACK LINE	
"	"	11.10pm	Message received from 2/Lt CAIN (OC P Battery Pink Armlet Column) "Have changed 16000 Rounds shell hole near UHLAN FARM. Could not go by No 5 Track owing to enemy shelling it with gas shells. Took ten runners from No 3 Section (i.e. P Battery). There men have joined their section. Not many information as to whereabouts of have dumped ammunition."	
"	31/7/17		Points from Section Diaries - Gunner was in front of their original front line now existent slight opposition encountered at JASPER FARM which was overcome by a rush, the Section officer Lt HANSEN - became mortally wounded. at 4pm two guns sent forward to BLACK LINE and took up position in shell holes E of POMMERN REDOUBT	No 1 Section Diary

A6945 Wt. W11422/M1160 350,000 12/16 D. D. & L. Forms/C/2118/14.

WAR DIARY
INTELLIGENCE SUMMARY
(Erase heading not required.)

Army Form C. 2118.

Place	Date	Hour	Summary of Events and Information	Remarks and references to Appendices
YPRES SALIENT (WIELTJE - WARWICK FARM SECTOR)	31/7/17	3.50a	At Zero there was practically no enemy barrage on first firing position of "P" Battery	No 2 & 3 Sections Diary
		5.13a	Barrage MG's ceased firing & prepared to advance to 2nd Barrage position. One holding officer & NCO went ahead of the battery to select the next (P2) Battery position & to put out aiming posts for the guns. They were fired on by a machine gun believed to be slightly N of POMMERN CASTLE	
		9.20a	Guns in position in P2 position & a test fired. No m.g. fire was encountered by the guns on coming forward & getting into position	
		10a	Position badly shelled - believed to be by some sort of Minenwerfer shell - several casualties resulting.	
		10.30a	Pack Mules carrying belt boxes arrived at about 10.30 a.m.	
		10.40a	P Battery commenced to move forward to P2 position - ground very heavy	
		11.15a	Guns mounted	
		12.10pm	Barrage fired completed. Guns then laid on SOS. lines for protection of GREEN LINE (164th Bde Objective). The proposed then dug in about 150 x W of POMMERN REDOUBT	
			Rain fell during the afternoon	
	31/7/17	4.20a	Advance commenced through the 7th & 9th Manyos which had the BLACKLINE (POMMERN REDOUBT) for objective.	No 4 Section
		5.5a	Passed BLUE LINE I (No casualties). One team whose gun had been forced in the assembly task	Diary

WAR DIARY
INTELLIGENCE SUMMARY
(Erase heading not required.)

Army Form C. 2118.

Place	Date	Hour	Summary of Events and Information	Remarks and references to Appendices
YPRES SALIENT	3/7/17	5.5 a.m.	Following in rear.	
	"	6 a.m.	Held up at APPLE VILLA by very strong sniping + m.g. fire from the ridge, half right of the advance.	No 4 Section
	"	6.30 a.m.	As the fire did not slacken the advance was resumed. 3 casualties from bullet wounds regarding	Strong
	"	7.30 a.m.	Reached Objective [BLACK LINE]. One gun placed on left flank firing N.W, one at N.E. corner of POMMERN REDOUBT firing N.W. The remaining two guns taken to centre of REDOUBT and pushed out to the Strong Point (under construction) N.E. of the REDOUBT) under heavy rifle fire from which no casualties resulted. The guns	
	"	9 a.m.	at N.E. corner of REDOUBT were subsequently withdrawn + moved to the centre firing N.W. when all guns were in position ammunition carriers were sent back to JASPER FARM but did not return until next night being unable to find ammunition for a considerable time.	For final gun permanence.
	"	10.10 a.m.	The two guns which were in position on the flanks of the forward Strong Point gave excellent covering fire during the advance of the 154 Bde. They kept down every rifle fire + caught a number (about 30) of enemy retiring from a trench on the top of the ridge.	Map attached to D.O. No 28.
	"	—	When the Strong Point the 164 Bde fell back from GREEN LINE the Strong Point became untenable owing to enfilade fire from both flanks, one gun being temporarily put out of action by rifle fire. When the Strong Point was evacuated the two guns were withdrawn + placed one on extreme right flank of the Bde line which opened weak but steady return on the centre of the front covering right front firing about S.E. by E.	

B Marano Capt
for O.C. 163rd M.G. Coy

SECRET   165TH MACHINE GUN COY   COPY No. 7
                          OPERATION ORDER No. 27.A

Reference Maps
  Trench Map St Julien
  Hazebrouck
  Belgium 28 N.W.   20th July 1917

1. This Company will relieve the 164th Machine Gun Company in the Right Sector of the Divisional Front on the night 21st/22nd July.

2. Dispositions of Sections will, so far as is known at present, be as follows:-

   NOS. 1 & 4 SECTIONS   at BEDOUIN CAMP
   No. 3 SECTION   — POTIJZE WOOD
   No. 2   "   — CANAL BANK.

3. Dispositions of No. 3 sections guns:-
   2 guns PROWSE FM.   (C.28.S. & C.28.A)
   1 gun   POTIJZE WOOD (I.4.1)
   1 "   POTIJZE ROAD (I.3.1).

   No. 2 SECTION'S GUNS
   1 gun   CONGREVE WALK (C.27.S).
   1 "   RAMPARTS   (I.8.4)
   1 "   KAAIE SALIENT (I.2.8).
   1 "   H.Q.

4. GUIDES. Arrangements will be notified later.

5. TAKING OVER. The usual trench stores will be taken over by Nos. 2 & 3 sections; Indirect Fire Schemes taken over and arrangements made to continue fire without interruption in accordance with programme. List of stores taken over to be forwarded to Coy Hqrs by 12 noon on the 22nd inst. Belt boxes will be taken over unless notification to the contrary is received.

6. SPARE PARTS. Nos. 2 & 3 sections. Spare parts boxes and spare barrels, with the exception of 1 barrel per section to be sent to the artificer prior departure for trenches.

7. RUNNERS. One spare man per each section will be taken into the trenches and after bringing "RELIEF COMPLETE" will be retained at Coy. Hqrs.

8. ENTRAINING PARTY for Omnibus Train will consist of LT. STRETCH, 2LT. CAIN, NOS. 1 and 4 sections, 9 men of HQrs section; together with 26 other ranks of T.M.B. This party will report to R.T.O ST. OMER at 6 am on 21st.
The following transport will proceed with above party and travel by the Omnibus Train
3 HORSES and MESS CART.

9. ENTRAINING OFFICER for Omnibus Train.
LT. STRETCH will report to R.T.O. ST. OMER at 6am on 21st. This Officer will have with him for the information of the R.T.O ST. OMER the detailed entraining states of the units entraining in the Omnibus Train.

10. Remainder of Company will parade at 7.30 am outside No. 2 sections billet to march to ST. OMER and will entrain by the 2nd. PERSONNEL train. To report to entraining Officer at 10.30 am.

11. EXTRA TRANSPORT
One lorry will be at H.Q. at 6 am to collect Officers' kits, mens packs, Orderly Room boxes, etc. A loading party of 1 N.C.O. & 5 men will be detailed by No. 2 section
A signaller will be detailed to meet a guide lorry from MORINGHEM CHURCH at 6 am.
L/CPL. CUMMINGS, 1 H.Q cook and storeman will travel with this lorry.

COPY No.1. O.C. No.1 SECTION
     No.2   " No. 2 "
     No.3   " No. 3 "
     No.4   " No. 4 "
     No.5   C.S.M.
     No.6   SPARE
     No.7   WAR DIARY
     No.8   FILE.

H.S. Ray
Major

OFFICER CMDG. 165 MACHINE GUN Coy

165th MACHINE GUN COY
OPERATION ORDER No 28   COPY No 14

Ref. Trench Maps. ST. JULIEN 5A 1/10000   July 1917.
                   ZONNEBEKE 5A   "

1. The 165th Inf Brigade is attacking with the 5th & 6th Kings L.R. followed by the 7th & 9th Kings L.R. respectively – 5th & 7th Kings on the right, 6th and 9th on the left.

2. Brigade frontage will be approximately from C.29.c.75.30 to C.29.a.00.28.

3. The final objective of the 5th & 6th Kings will be the BLUE LINE, C.30.a.60.25 to C.23.d.70.40.
   The final objective of the 7th and 9th Kings will be the BLACK LINE, C.19.c.75.85 to C.24.b.55.70.

4. The ARTILLERY BARRAGE will start at ZERO on the GERMAN FRONT LINE.
   At ZERO plus 6 it will lift to the SUPPORT LINE and at ZERO + 10 on to the RESERVE LINE. The Barrage after clearing the front trench system will creep back at the rate of 100 yards in four minutes.
   On the Infantry reaching the BLUE LINE the Artillery will form a protective barrage 300 yards in front. This Barrage will come forward at ZERO plus 1 hour 23 minutes and creep at the rate of 100 yards in four minutes until the Infantry have reached the BLACK LINE, when it will again form a protective barrage about 300 yards in front.

5. EMPLOYMENT OF GUNS.
   Nos. 2 & 3 sections and A & B sections of the 196 M.G.Coy will be employed for Barrage work.
   No. 1 section will operate with 5th & 6th Kings L.R.
   No. 4 section will operate with the 7th & 9th Kings L.R.

- 2 -

6. MACHINE GUN BARRAGE

Nos. 2 & 3 sections will be referred to as "P Battery", and A & B sections of 196 M.Gy. as "Q Battery" in connection with the Barrage operations, and will be employed:-

(a) To cover the Infantry advance to the BLUE LINE.
(b) To keep the FREZENBERG LINE under fire during the pause on the BLUE LINE.
(c) To support the advance to the BLACK LINE at the commencement.
(d) To cover the Final Divisional Objective (GREEN LINE) with a S.O.S barrage.

P and Q Batteries will carry out the Barrage Scheme as laid down in separate orders.

Directly after the conclusion of the firing from the first position 1 Officer and 1 N.C.O from each Battery will move to the nearest Brigade Forward Station and ascertain the situation in front. They will then choose positions for their Batteries in accordance with the information received, and assist in guiding their Batteries to them. Before Batteries advance from P and Q to P.1 and Q.1 positions the guns must be cleaned and oiled up, barrels replaced if required, belts filled, and everything got ready for the advance, as early as possible.

The move to P.1 and Q.1 positions to be completed by ZERO + 5 hours 20 mins.

The move from P1 & Q1 to P.2 & Q.2 positions to be completed by ZERO + 7 hours 32 mins. As this only gives 42 minutes from "Cease fire" at P1 and Q1 positions the battery positions at P.2 and Q.2 must be selected, and ground pegged for gun positions, as early as possible.

7. DISPOSITION OF REMAINDER OF GUNS.

No.1 section (4 guns) will follow the Third

3.

wave of the troops to the GERMAN RESERVE LINE and will halt there until the BLUE LINE is consolidated, but may take up their positions in the BLUE LINE, at the discretion of Section Officers, before consolidation is completed.

These guns are detailed to take up the following positions :-

(a) STRONG POINT, near Southern Brigade Boundary firing N.E.
(b) CAMEL AVENUE, near the BLUE LINE, firing N.
(c) JASPER FARM.
(d) STRONG POINT C.23.d.80.20 (CAMBRAI DRIVE)

During the subsequent advance of the 7th Kings L.R. and 9th Kings L.R. these guns will cover the advance of the Infantry until they have passed the BLUE LINE, by bringing fire to bear on any German machine guns which open fire.

No. 4 section (4 guns) will move forward with the troops attacking the BLACK LINE, two guns with the fourth wave of the 7th K.L.R. and two with the fourth wave of the 9th K.L.R., but will halt at the BLUE LINE until the BLACK LINE has been captured, and is being consolidated, or may move forward at the discretion of the Section Officer, before consolidation is completed.

These guns will occupy the following points in the BLACK LINE :-

(a) Two guns in the STRONG POINT on the spur S.W. of GALLIPOLI.
(b) About D.19.a.50.42.
(c) About C.24.b.95.46.

8. A strong point will be made by the R.E. at about D.19.c.05.60 and will be garrisoned by half a platoon and a Lewis gun from the 7th Kings, and one machine gun from No. 1 section (BLUE LINE).

9. S.O.S. Signal will be the Rifle Grenade pattern bursting into two Red and two Green Lights.

10. AMMUNITION

P and Q Batteries. Each Battery will take 8 Belt boxes per gun to P and Q positions respectively. A dump of 75 extra belt boxes will be made by each Battery at PROWSE FARM.

Six pack animals per Battery will be employed to carry ammunition from P and Q positions to P.1, Q.1, and P.2, Q.2, positions, but carriers must also be used by Battery Commanders to assist in this work.

Each Battery's pack animals must be in command of an Officer and he will be responsible for maintaining the supply of ammunition to the Battery.

Dumps will be formed at suitable advanced positions at about C.24.C.80.70 and C.24.b.60.30.

Nos. 1 and 4 SECTIONS must depend on their Ammunition Carriers until P. Battery has been fully supplied with Ammunition.

11. AMMUNITION DUMPS.

A Brigade S.A.A. dump will be formed at PLUM FARM of 300,000 rounds as soon as possible after the BLACK LINE has been captured.

S.A.A dumps for use of P & Q Batteries have been formed at :-

C.28.d.20.10 (behind P. Battery) 60,000
C.28.c.95.20 (" Q ") 60,000
C.28.c.75.40 (For use of P & Q Batteries) 312,000

A S.A.A dump of 20,000 rounds has been formed at PROWSE FARM for the use of Nos. 1 and 4 sections, if required.

5

BATTALION DUMPS, containing SAA, Bombs Water, R.E material, have been established as follows:-
(a) Junction of FRONT LINE and the STRAND.
(b) "   "   "   "   "   PAGODA TRENCH.
(c) "   "   "   SECOND TRENCH and STRAND.
(d) "   "   "   "   "   PAGODA TRENCH

The Brigade dump is at POTIZZE CHATEAU.

12. SALVAGE.   No damage is to be done to captured guns or machine guns, unless there appears to be a likelihood of their re-capture by the enemy.
All papers, maps etc. which may be found in dugouts or on German Officers will be collected and sent to Brigade Headquarters.

13. PRISONERS.   No personal effects, such as decorations, watches, identity discs, paybooks, mess tins, waterbottles, haversacks, or spoons & forks, will be taken from the prisoners.

14. MEDICAL.   Regimental Aid posts will be established at C.28.d.6.7 in PAGODA TRENCH. The advanced Dressing Station will be at I.1.b.9.3 (CANAL BANK) Collecting Posts will be at C.27.d.3.1 and at POTIZZE (I.u.a.7.3)
WALKING WOUNDED will proceed via PAGODA TRENCH, or one of the trenches, to the collecting post at POTIZZE.

15. TRAFFIC.   After ZERO the STRAND will be an up trench and PAGODA a down trench.
If the enemy's artillery fire is not heavy all movement after ZERO will be over the top.

16.   The Hour of ZERO will be notified later.

bNarrono Capt
for
OFFICER CMDG 165 Machine Gun Coy

Copy No. 1 — O.C. No. 1 Section
" " 2 — " No. 2 "
" " 3 — " No. 3 "
" " 4 — " No. 4 "
" " 5 — O.C. 1st Battery
" " 6 — O.C. "Q" "
" " 7 — O.C. A Section. 196 M.G. Coy
" " 8 — O.C. B " "
" " 9 — O.C. Transport
" " 10 — 2nd Lt. W.H. Cain
" " 11 — C.O.
" " 12 — 2nd I/C
" " 13 — File
" " 14 — War Diary
" " 15 — Spare.

SECRET

165th MACHINE GUN COMPANY
OPERATION ORDER No. 26

COPY No. 7

Ref Maps. - Trench Maps Belgium Sheet 28 N.W
Hazebrouck 1/100000 1/20000

1st July 1917

1. The 165th Machine Gun Company will be relieved in the line by the 164th Machine Gun Company on the night 2nd/3rd. July.

2. GUIDES. May not be required. If required arrangements will be notified later.

3. HANDING OVER.

   (a) All trench stores and belt boxes will be handed over and receipts taken. The receipts will be handed in to Orderly Room by 9 am on the 3rd. inst.

   (b) The receipts must show in addition to the usual Trench stores, all furniture, such as beds, tables, latrine boxes, etc., The Range Boards, Sentry Order Boards, and other emplacement boards. Separate receipts to be obtained for belt boxes.

   (c) Fire programmes will be handed over to the relieving Officers, together with records of firing from 6am on the 2nd. July. Indirect fire positions will be handed over and suitable arrangements made to enable the fire programme to be continued without interruption by the relief.

   (d) All work in progress and contemplated will be handed over in writing.

4. All Camp Kettles, & cooking gear, the property of this Company, will be returned to Coy. Hqrs as early as possible on the 2nd. July.

5. PACKING OF LIMBERS.

   In order to have Transport free to move early on the morning of the 3rd., the following will be responsible for packing their section's limbers:- No. 1 Section - Sgt. Wroe. No. 2 Section - Sgt. Kemp. No. 3 Section - L/Cpl. Wylie. No. 4 Section - Sgt. Winrow. Section limbers will be properly packed by 6am. on the 3rd., unless otherwise ordered by Transport Officer.

-2-

6. Attached men of 9th K.L.R. will proceed to Transport lines under Sgt. Kemp during the afternoon of the 2nd. July, leaving Coy HQrs at 2:30 pm.

7. No.1 Section will proceed under Section Sergeant to Transport lines during the afternoon of the 2nd. July, guns and tripods being carried on pack animals. Section Sergeant will see to the packing of Section limbers, ready for move on the following day, before 6am on the 3rd. inst.

8. TRANSPORT. Will be required as follows:-
At 3pm on 2nd. inst — 4 pack animals for guns and tripods of No.1 section.
Other requirements will be notified later.

9. REPORTS. Completion of relief will be notified to Coy. HQrs. by each O.C. Section as soon as possible. The runners used for this purpose will proceed to billets with HQrs. party.

10. RETURN TO BILLETS
(a) TRANSPORT. All transport will return direct to Transport lines, with the exception of the Mess Cart and HQrs limber, which will proceed to RED ROSE CAMP, BRANDHOEK to unload before returning to Transport lines.

(b) Sections will proceed independently by Route march to RED ROSE CAMP, BRANDHOEK (H.1.6.8.2.)

11. Lt. Ramage has been detailed to take over above Camp and will be responsible for providing each party with accommodation on arrival.

12. The Company (less mounted portion) will proceed by train from POPERINGHE on the 3rd. July, probably to ST. OMER, and will thence march to BOISDINGHEM AREA. They will be met by the billeting party and conducted to the Company Billets.

3.

13. The Transport will move on the 3rd July to BOISDINGHEM AREA, (halting for the night 3rd/4th at WALLON CAPEL) with the remainder of Brigade Transport, by Route march, under the orders of the Brigade Transport Officer. Move to be complete by 10 am.

   LT. BRAY will accompany 2 LT. COUTTS on this move.

```
Copy No. 1    O.C. No. 1 SECTION
  "   "  2     "   "  2    "
       3      "   "  3    "
       4      "   "  4    "
       5      "  TRANSPORT
       6     FILE
       7     WAR DIARY
       8     C.S.M
       9     SPARE
```

b Parsons Lt
for O.C. 165 MACHINE GUN Coy

SECRET   165TH MACHINE GUN COY.   COPY No. 5

APPENDIX A TO OPERATION ORDER No. 28

REF. MAPS. ST. JULIEN } 1/10000   July 1917.
            ZONNEBEKE

PACK ANIMALS

1. Ammunition for P and Q Batteries, which will form the Machine Gun Barrage, will be taken forward on Pack Animals from the dumps at P and Q positions, to P1, Q1 and P2, Q2 positions.

2. Six Pack Animals per Battery will be employed under the command of an Officer, assisted by a Lance Corporal; each animal to have a man with it. These Pack Animals will in future be referred to as "P and Q Battery Ammunition Columns".

3. Each animal will be equipped with a pack saddle to carry Belt boxes, or S.A.A. boxes, a Gas Helmet, and a day's feed; and each column will also carry 3 water buckets, 2 shovels and 2 picks.

     The Officer, N.C.O and men will be equipped in fighting order, with two Iron rations, and the unexpended portion of the day's rations.

     The N.C.O. will also carry a pair of wire cutters.

4. DUMPS to draw ammunition from.
     The ammunition dumps have been formed at the following places:—
     (a) PROWSE FARM (C.28.d.35.2)   100 Belt boxes.
     (b)   (C.28.c.75.40)   300,000 rds S.A.A.

5. TRACKS.
     No. 4 Track which passes just to the SOUTH of PROWSE FARM will be continued and will be marked out by white posts and the German trenches bridged or filled in. This track will run close to UHLAN FARM, as far as the BLUE LINE. A continuation of this track will be made from the BLUE LINE about C.30.a.02.99 passing just NORTH of PLUM FARM to POMMERN CASTLE (D.19.a.25.20.).

     No. 5 Track (alternate route) which runs to the NORTH of PAGODA TR. will be continued from OXFORD TR. to the BLUE LINE at a point where the latter cuts CAMBRAI AVENUE. This track will be continued to the BLACK LINE and will pass just NORTH of BANK FARM.

- 2 -

6. BATTERY LOCATIONS

(a) From Z until Z + 1 hr 25 mins :-
   P Position - C.28.d.46.18 (PROWSE FARM).
   Q   "   - C.28.d.18.32   "   "

(b) From Z + 5 hrs 20 mins to Z + 6 hrs 50 mins :-
   P.1.   - C.24.c.95.68 (NE. PLUM FARM)
   Q1.   - C.24.a.61.11   "   "   "

(c) From Z + 7 hrs 32 mins :-
   P.2   - D.19.a.04.34 (POMMERN CASTLE)
   Q2.   - C.24.b.9.8 (N " ")

7. FORWARD DUMPS. Forward dumps to be made at the following locations :-

   C.24.c.80.75   for P.1, Q1 Battery positions.
   C.24.b.36.20   for P.2, Q2 " "

8. DIRECTIONS.

No. 4 TRACK.
From PROWSE FARM to UHLAN FARM, - 54° TRUE = 67° MAG.
  " UHLAN FARM to just N of PLUM F^M - 51° " = 64° "
  " PLUM FARM to POMMERN CASTLE - 68° " = 81° "

No. 5 TRACK.
From OXFORD TR to GERMAN SUPPORT LINE - 36° TRUE = 49° MAG.
  " GERMAN SUPPORT LINE through BLUE LINE to BLACK LINE } - 58° TRUE = 71° MAG.

                          C Parsons Capt
                     for
                  OFFICER CMMDG. 165 Machine Gun Coy

Copy No. 1 - O.C. Transport.
  " " 2 - O.C. P Battery Amm. Column
  " " 3 - O.C. Q " "
  " " 4 - File
  " " 5 - War Diary
  " " 6 - } Spare
  " " 7 - }

SECRET   165 MACHINE GUN COMPANY   Copy No. 4.
OPERATION ORDER NO. 27 B
Ref:- TRENCH MAP. ST JULIEN.   1st July

1. At 11 p.m tonight a shrapnel barrage will open on NO MAN'S LAND 50 yds in front of our own wire. This will gradually creep back at intervals to the GERMAN FRONT LINE. It will then die away. Frontage C.29.a.70.57 to C.29.a.40.72.

2. STOKES MORTARS will fire on WHITE SAP during the bombardment, and the ground between our own front line & the shrapnel barrage will be searched with rifle grenades.

3. After enemy's barrage has slackened a patrol of 6th Kings will search NO MAN'S LAND for identifications.

4. Three machine guns of this Company will co-operate as follows:—

(A) Under 2/Lt BROWN
- ENGLISH FARM gun will fire from THE ADNEGOLE ST at a position approx. above I of ENGLISH FARM.
- C.27.4 gun will fire from LIVERPOOL TR. at a position approx. C.27.d.30.95.

(b) Under 2/Lt BLACK — C.27.5 gun will fire from JUNCTION ROAD at above road junction I.3.b.40.65

Each of the above guns will traverse along

a line from C.29.a.28.72 to C.29.a.65.45 so as to sweep GERMAN WIRE and ground in front of his front line trench

5. TIME and DURATION of FIRE – Fire will be opened at 11 p.m and will last until 11.10 p.m.

6. Lewis guns will be assisting the machine guns in searching NO MAN'S LAND.

Copy No 1 – O.C. No 2 Section
  "   " 2 – "   " 4 "
  "   " 3 – FILE.
  "   " 4 – WAR DIARY.

F R Parsons Lt
for O.C. 165 M.G. Coy.

To accompany 55th Division No. M.O. 204 (a).

PROGRAMME OF MOVES.

Division.	Battery.	Moves.	Remarks.
55th	P	Advance to P1 at Zero + 1 hr 25 mins. Move to be completed by Zero + 4 hrs 20 mins.	Guns must not advance E of the BLUE objective until the Infantry have captured the BLACK line In the event of the Infantry being held up W of the FREZENBURG Line guns will get into action about the BLUE line to support the Infantry with overhead fire.
	Q	Advance to Q1 at Zero + 1 hr 25 mins. Move to be completed by Zero + 4 hrs 20 mins.	Guns must not advance E of the BLUE objective until the Infantry have captured the BLACK line In the event of the Infantry being held up W of the FREZENBURG line guns will get into action about the BLUE line to support the Infantry with overhead fire.
	R	Advance to R1 at Zero + 1 hr 25 mins. Move to be completed by Zero + 4 hrs 20 mins.	Guns must not advance E of the BLUE objective until the Infantry have captured the BLACK LINE. In the event of the Infantry being held up W of the FREZENBURG line guns will get into action about the BLUE line to support the Infantry with overhead fire.
	S	Advance to S1 at Zero + 1 hr 25 mins. Move to be completed by Zero + 4 hrs 20 mins.	Guns must not advance E of the BLUE Objective until the Infantry have captured the BLACK line. In the event of the Infantry being held up W of the FREZENBURG line guns will get into action about the BLUE line to support the Infantry with overhead fire.

To accompany 55th Division No. M.O. 204 (a).

PROGRAMME OF MOVES.

Division.	Battery.	Moves.	Remarks.
55th [hand] 165th MGCoy	P1	Advance to P2 at Zero + 6 hrs 50 mins. Move to be completed by Zero + 7 hrs 32 mins.	
	Q1	Advance to Q2 at Zero + 6 hrs 50 mins. Move to be completed by Zero + 7 hrs 32 mins.	
	R1	Advance to R2 at Zero + 6 hrs 50 mins. Move to be completed by Zero + 7 hrs 32 mins.	
	S1	Advance to S2 at Zero + 6 hrs 50 mins. Move to be completed by Zero + 7 hrs 32 mins.	

8 | 4 Sur Terre / 2 Caissons /   Section: 8 caissons 1820

Coy. H.Q

To accompany 55th Division No. M.O. 204 (G).

M.G. FIRE ORGANIZATION ORDER.

No of group or Batty.	No of guns.	Composition.	Commander.	Location.	Firing From	Firing to	TARGET.	Rate of Fire.	Remarks.
Q	8	196 M.G. Coy.		C.28.d.18.32	0	18	C.24.c.67.32 to C.24.a.22.02	1 belt per 4 mins.	Search 300 yds beyond Target. Depression Stops to be set for Q.E. of Target.
					19	1.5	C.24.b.52.12 to C.24.a.83.76	1 belt per 4 mins.	Search 200 yds beyond Target. Depression Stops to be set for Q.E. of Target. On S.O.S. open maximum rate for 10 mins and continue ordinary rate after.
					1.6	1.23	C.24.b.64.36 to C.18.d.19.00	1 belt per 4 mins.	Depression Stops to be set for Q.E. of Target.

To accompany 55th Division No. M.O. 204 (G).

M.G. FIRE ORGANIZATION ORDER.

No of group or Btty.	No of guns.	Composition.	Commander.	Location.	Firing From	to	TARGET.	Rate of Fire.	Remarks.
Q1	8	196 M.G. Coy.		O.24.a.61.11			D.13.d.99.65 to D.13.b.64.38		Fire one belt as soon as in position. On S.O.S. open maximum rate of fire for 10 mins and continue ordinary rate of fire for 5 mins.
					6.08	6.32	D.13.d.99.65 to D.13.b.64.38	1 belt per 4 mins.	Search 300 yds beyond Target. Depression Stops to be set for Q.E. of Target.
					6.33	6.50	D.14.a.67.06 to D.14.a.53.84	1 belt per 4 mins.	Search 300 yds beyond Target. Depression Stops to be set for Q.E. of Target.

To accompany 55th Division No. M.O. 204 (G).

M.G. FIRE ORGANIZATION ORDER.

No of group or Batty.	No of guns.	Composition.	Commander.	Location.	Firing From	to	TARGET.	Rate of Fire.	Remarks.
Q2	8	196 M.G. Coy.		C.24.b.9.8	7.32	8.20	D.9.c.30.14 to D.8.d.94.84	1 belt per 4 mins.	Maintain fire for half an hour. Search 200 yds beyond targets. Depression Stops to be set for Q.E. of target. On S.O.S. maximum rate of fire to be opened on targets and maintained for 10 mins and then continue at ordinary rate for 5 mins.

MACHINE GUN COMPANY.

No. of Gun S.1.8.

N.C.O. i/c ....; No. 1 ....

	TIME From	To.	QUADRANT ELEVATION	DIRECTION Magnetic	NO: OF BELTS	REMARKS.
Q.	0	1.8	4°25'–6°15'	76°–62°	5	Search 300^x
	1.9	1h5	7°15'–9°0'	67°–58°	12	Search 300^x SOS max 10 min + ordinary rate
	1h6	1h23	9°30'	67°–58°	5	
Q1.						
	4h20	4h24	3°35'	76°–65°	1	SOS max 10 min + ord. rate for 5 min
	6h08	6h32	3°35'–5°5'	76°–65°	6	Search 300^x
	6h33	6h50	5°55'–8°0'	76°–65°	5	" 300^x
Q2.	7h32	8h20	7°45'–9°25'	76°–64°	12	SOS max 10 min + ord. rate 5 min Search 300^x

P. BATT.   LEFT HALF BATT.

BARRAGE CARD

GUN POS.	TIME	(MAG) DIRECTION	ELEVATION & SEARCHING	RATE OF FIRE	REMARKS
P	0 - 18	72° - 68°	4°-0' to 5°-02'	250 RDS per 4 MIN.	S.O.S. MAX RATE
P	19 - 1.5	69° - 66°	6°-30' to 9°-10'	- " -	10 MIN. THEN
P	1.6 - 1.23	69° - 66°	9°-37' to 10°-30'	- " -	ORDINARY RATE
DIRECTION OF ADVANCE 68° MAG. MOVE COMPLETED ZERO + 5-20					
P1	WHEN GUN MOUNTED 1 BELT	76° - 71°	3°-24'	ONE BELT	
P1	6.08 - 6.32	76° - 71°	3°-24' to 4°-47'	250 RDS per 4 MIN	-do- -do-
P1	6.33 - 6.50	75° - 71°	5°-20' to 7°-20'	-do-	-do- -do- FOR 5 MIN
DIRECTION OF ADVANCE 83° MAG. MOVE COMPLETED ZERO + 7.32					
P2	7.32 - 8.20	75° - 70°	7°-25' to 9°-10'	-do-	-do- -do- FOR 5 MIN

"P" Batt.   **BARRAGE CARD**   Right Half Batt.

Gun Position	Time	(Mag) Direction	Elevation & Searching	Rate of Fire	Remarks
P	0 – 18	78° – 73°	3°-57' to 5°-0'	250 rds per 4 mins	S.O.S Max Rate
P	19 – 1.5	74° – 70°	6°-33' to 9°-10'	– " –	10 MIN. THEN
P	1.6 – 1.23	74° – 70°	10°-20' to 11°-15'	– " –	ORDINARY RATE.

Direction of Advance 68° Mag. Move Completed Zero + 5-20

P1	When Gun Mounted 1 Belt	82° – 77°	3° – 3¼'	One Belt	
P1	6.08 – 6.32	82° – 77°	3°-34' to 4°-50'	250 rds per 4 min.	– do –
P1	6.33 – 6.50	80° – 76°	5°-0' to 7°-0'	– " –	– do – for 5 min

Direction of Advance 83° Mag. Move Completed Zero + 7.32

| P2 | 7.32 – 8.20 | 78° – 74° | 7°-25' to 9°-10' | – " – | – do – for 5 min. |

Coy. H.Q.

To accompany 55th Division No. M.O. 204 (a).

M.G. FIRE ORGANIZATION ORDER.

No of group or Batty.	No of guns.	Composition.	Commander.	Location.	Firing From	Firing to	TARGET.	Rate of Fire.	Remarks.
P	8	165 M.G. Coy.		C.28.d.45.18	0	18	C.30.b.00.75 to C.24.c.60.43	1 belt per 4 mins.	Search 200 yds beyond Target. Depression Stops to be set for Q.E. of Target.
					19	1.5	C.24.d.71.42 to C.24.b.32.12	1 belt per 4 mins.	Search 300 yds beyond Target. Depression Stops to be set for Q.E. of Target. On S.O.S. maximum rate to be opened on Target for 10 mins and continue ordinary rate after.
					1.6	1.23	D.19.c.41.88 to C.24.b.83.48	1 belt per 4 mins.	Search 100 yds beyond Target. Depression Stops to be set for Q.E. of Target.

To accompany 55th Division No. M.O. 204 (G).

M.G. FIRE ORGANIZATION ORDER.

No of group or Batty.	No of guns.	Composition.	Commander.	Location.	TARGET. Firing From	to	TARGET.	Rate of Fire.	Remarks.
P1	8	165 M.G. Coy.		C.24.c.95.68.			D.20.a.35.95 to D.13.d.99.65		Fire one belt as soon as in position. On S.O.S. open maximum rate of fire for 10 mins and continue ordinary rate of fire for 5 mins.
					6.08	6.32	D.20.a.35.95 to D.13.d.99.65	1 belt per 4 mins	Search 300 yds beyond Target. Depression Stops to be set for Q.E. of Target.
					6.33	6.50	D.14.c.93.30 to D.14.a.67.06	1 belt per 4 mins	Search 300 yds beyond Target. Depression Stops to be set for Q.E. of Target.

To accompany 55th Division No. M.O. 204 (a).

M.G. FIRE ORGANIZATION ORDER.

No of group or batty.	No of guns.	Composition.	Commander.	Location.	Firing From to	TARGET.	Rate of Fire.	Remarks.
P2	8	165 M.G. Coy.		D.19.a.04.34	7.32 to 8.20	D.15.a.62.40 to D.9.c.20.10	1 belt per 4 mins.	Maintain fire for half an hour. Search 200 yds beyond targets. Depression Stops to be set for Q.E. of Target. On S.O.S. maximum rate of fire to be opened on target and maintained for 10 mins and then continue at ordinary rate for 5 mins.

War Diary
of
165th M. G. Coy
for period
1st to 31st August, 1917.

Army Form C. 2118.

WAR DIARY
or
INTELLIGENCE SUMMARY.
(Erase heading not required.)

Instructions regarding War Diaries and Intelligence Summaries are contained in F. S. Regs., Part II. and the Staff Manual respectively. Title pages will be prepared in manuscript.

Place	Date	Hour	Summary of Events and Information	Remarks and references to Appendices
YPRES SALIENT (WIELTJE SECTOR)	1/8/17	9.10am	OC received message from OC P Battery (LT RAMAGE) asking for ammunition and (?) a list of casualties	A
"	"	12 noon	Following message sent to OC "P Battery" & OC "Q Battery":- "You will withdraw your Battery to a position at about C.30.a.37.60 in BLUE LINE. Prior to dispatch in our of 805 m Barrage line D.19.b.85.60 to D.15.c.75.60. P battery will move half an hour on receipt of message and Q Battery on receipt of message. The Battery will have no much ammunition as possible with it. No 4 Section has keep plenty of SAA in the BLUE LINE you Returns will be brought up to the BLUE LINE	
"	"	12.40pm	Following Message received from MC O Ye No 1 Section (BLUE LINE) giving position (?) and casualties when this message also stated - "Situation - Very heavy artillery fire against our front line last night. This morning situation quiet up to time of dispatch when enemy artillery again became active. State of tracks very bad. We had a limped put out of action but discount team which the 190* Coy not refunded, so replaced the damaged one."	NOTE It appears that message to Q Battery was not delivered as been standing by in the event
"	"	3.30pm	A message dispatched from OC P Battery at 2.30 pm was received, acknowledging instructions to move to BLUE LINE and reporting - "Am leaving one team with Lt STRETCH (OC No.4) as he is short of men. "O" the GREEN LINE has been evacuated we have merely been standing by in the event of a counter attack Strength of P Battery 41 men"	nothing left of team AR

A 6945. Wt. W.14422/M.1160. 350,000. 12/16. D, D. & L. Form/C./2118/14.

Army Form C. 2118.

WAR DIARY
INTELLIGENCE SUMMARY
(Erase heading not required.)

Place	Date	Hour	Summary of Events and Information	Remarks and references to Appendices
YPRES SALIENT (WIELTJE SECTOR)	1/8/17	8 p.m.	Following message received from O.C. No 2 Section (P.Bentley) - "I have at present 20 men under my command. One gun of No 2 Section and one of No 3 being under Lt. Pritchet at the BLACK LINE. The figures above include both 2 & 3 sections. The men are reduced to the stem and their morale has greatly deteriorated owing to extremely heavy shell fire and the large proportion of casualties (over 50%). L. Ramage who remained at the BLACK LINE to source barrage fire has not yet turned up. L. Scanes has reported to me - one of no 4 will always be at URBAN FARM. All are worn out both as regards morale and physical condition."	NOTE A On writing these men next morning O.C. found them very cheery, brighter after a few words, & all said they would stick it
"	"	8 p.m.	O.C. also received following message from O.C. No 4 Section this message having been sent off at 2 p.m. - "I sent you a message yesterday from POMMERN CASTLE at 8.15 a.m. Fire guns not in firing condition - worked so much I could do with 2000 SAA. Have three very badly wounded men and cannot get them evacuated. No S.B. Casualties 1 Killed, 9 wounded, 2 missing." In consequence of this message orders were given for the ration party to take up stretchers to evacuate the badly wounded men and that in fact a ration parties were always to take up stretchers and assist anyone down who needed it.	NOTE Prior to receipt of this message P.O.C. had already ordered Pt P.G. Pattinson to hunt over all SAA in No 4 Section.
"	2/8/17	9.30 a.m.	O.C. made tour of BLUE LINE & found stretchers & men in very bad condition although were the circumstances the men were very cheery. N.C.O. i/c No 1 Section reported that he had plenty of SAA but was rather short of bullets & bell bosses.	

Army Form C. 2118.

Instructions regarding War Diaries and Intelligence Summaries are contained in F. S. Regs., Part II. and the Staff Manual respectively. Title pages will be prepared in manuscript.

WAR DIARY
INTELLIGENCE SUMMARY.
(Erase heading not required.)

Place	Date	Hour	Summary of Events and Information	Remarks and references to Appendices
YPRES SALIENT (WIELTJE SECTOR)	2/8/17	—	On return from trenches O.C. found a message from N.C.O. i/c No1 Section which warned him for the trenches. — "The trenches in which my guns are have been shelled very heavily for the last 24 hours at regular intervals. Confusion was caused at 4.20 p.m. yesterday by a report that our advanced lines were retreating. The infantry holding the BLUE LINE on the left flank retired to OLD German Reserve Trench and ordered my guns to retire. Going out to see what happened I met my gun teams and sent them back to the BLUE LINE not knowing the situation was bad about that time on Nov 2 & 7. Frontierways was going on my right and left but situation was bad about the time on Nov 28. 3 Sections (P. Battery) were coming back to take up positions in the BLUE LINE and might have caused the idea of troops retiring from the BLACK LINE. — No further causalities to report. All guns in same positions. Pending order I return received also OL 24.V.32. Returns have been sent to respective sections."	←
"	"	8 p.m.	Following message sent off to O.C. No 4 Section — "Extra guns are being sent to you of the 107th Coy but you will not be relieved until the 107th Bde H.Qrs are satisfied they can hold the line with their own guns. C.S.M is taking a party over to you at daylight tomorrow morning with your rations and three stretchers and will bring back your three worst cases."	
"	"	8.10 p.m	Message received from O.C. No 4 Section as follows :— "The positions of my guns are shown on the attached	

BP

WAR DIARY
INTELLIGENCE SUMMARY
(Erase heading not required.)

Army Form C. 2118.

Place	Date	Hour	Summary of Events and Information	Remarks and references to Appendices
YPRES SALIENT (WIELTJE SECTOR)	2/8/17	—	map. Could you possibly send up by the runner some RUM and CANDLES. My HQrs are in the front line at present. 1 LA Lg no. with B Coy. 1st ALR. Both some arrangements held good for rations if so I will send at dawn as today. Casualties - 1 killed, 1 died of wounds, 9 wounded, 1 missing.	← 2/8/17 night
"	"	10 pm	O.C. 107th M.G. Coy reported at Batt. HQrs for guides to take his 2 sections to BLUE LINE and POMMERN REDOUBT.	2 Coys all day ?
"	"	10.15 pm	He left Batt HQrs with his guides. the O.C. Section of 107th Coy then knew he was not to relieve our No 4 Section until he received orders from his own Coy Commander. Other Section of 107th Coy was to reinforce barrage gunn in BLUE LINE	← Raining
"	3/8/17	9 a.m	O.C. No. 4 reported that he had been relieved by the O.C Section of 107th M.G Coy sent to reinforce him, he reporting to O.C No. 4 Section that he was quite able to hold the line with his own guns. O.C No. 4 Section left all his ammunition on relief in POMMERN REDOUBT and was brought out only by great initiative. Batt. HQrs. of 1/6th & 1/07th Bnn were at once notified that No.4 Section had been relieved and at 11 am 107th O'Bnn were satisfied with the position at POMMERN REDOUBT.	Raining
"	"	9.30 am	message received from NCO I/c No 1 Section " 2 Sections of 107th M.G Coy arrived JASPER FARM at 4.30 am. One Section went on to relieve No 4 Section, the other took up Barrage Position " Enemy Paid particular attention to BLUE LINE yesterday shelling very heavy at times. At 5 pm a heavy bombardment	← Raining

EP

WAR DIARY
INTELLIGENCE SUMMARY
(Erase heading not required.)

Army Form C. 2118.

Place	Date	Hour	Summary of Events and Information	Remarks and references to Appendices
YPRES SALIENT (WIELTJE SECTOR)	3/8/17 (cont)		of enemies lines now right. This seemed to ease up the shelling of BLUE LINE a very little. Was heard of enemys attacking for some time after. Bombardment was again heavy at 9.30 p.m and a great number of red green & yellow Very lights were sent up by enemy on a very wide front but nothing further under the barrage. Enemy again shelled BLUE LINE at 4.30 a.m this morning but our artillery replied effectively.	heavy to very heavy ← shower of rain
"	4/8/17	11 am	The 1,2 & 3 Sections returned to the 108th M.G Coy and proceeded via YPRES POPERINGHE	
POPERINGHE	5/8/17		The 1,2 & 3 Sections at POPERINGHE Transport still y.Section in huts near WATOU	
"	6/8/17	4 am	Transport moved off by Route March for RECQUES Area	
"	"	11 am	Dismounted portion of Company entrained at ABEELE for RECQUES AREA. & arrived at AUDRICQ Station conveyed by lorries to billets at NIELLES-LEZ-ARDRES	
	7/8/17 to 31/8/17		Refitting and Training of Company. Reinforcements received bringing the Company up to strength	

S.P. Watson Capt
for O.C. 165th M.G Coy.

CONFIDENTIAL

165/5/5

WM 20

WAR DIARY
OF
165. M.G. COY.
FOR PERIOD
1/9/17 – 30/9/17

WAR DIARY / INTELLIGENCE SUMMARY

Army Form C. 2118.

Place	Date	Hour	Summary of Events and Information	Remarks and references to Appendices
NIELLES- LEZ-ARDRES	1/9/17 to 12/9/17		Training etc. on usual lines	
"	13/9/17	3pm	Operation Order No 30 for move to forward Area issued	O.O No 30 attached
"	14/9/17	7.30am	Transport commenced move to Forward Area in accordance with O.O No 30.	
"	15/9/17	1.45pm	Remainder of Company left AUDRUICQ STATION for PESELHOEK in accordance with O.O No 30	
YPRES SALIENT	"	10.30pm	Arrived at PESELHOEK SIDING and proceeded to bivouac camp in VLAMERTINGHE No 2 Area	
"	16/9/17	—	Preparation for forthcoming attack.	
"	17/9/17	4pm	Operation Order No 31 for forthcoming attack issued. Intermittent shelling of camp area by day & night. By his long range H.V. gun. No casualties.	O.O No 31 attached
"	"	6.30pm	Nos 1 & 2 Sections moved up to Swan in WIELTJE SECTOR and took up position in ST JEAN. No guns in action.	Amendment to O.O No 31 issued
"	18/9/17	12 noon	Amendment A to O.O No 31 issued	Amendment to O.O. No 31 attached
"	18/9/17	4pm	Nos 1 & 2 Section relieved two Sections of 116. M.G. Coy. in position in forward lines	
"	18/9/17	6.30pm	No. 3 & 4 Section left VLAMERTINGHE No 2. AREA for our concentration position in ST JEAN.	
"	18/9/17	4.30pm	Coy. H.Qrs. left VLAMERTINGHE No 2 AREA for forward Co.H.Qrs position with Batt. H.Qrs in WIELTJE.	
"	19/9/17	7pm	Sections fixed up in assembly positions with the Reserve Companies of Battns with which they were to go over with	
(WIELTJE SECTOR)		4?		
"	20/9/17	5.40am	ZERO HOUR. Attacking troops moved forward in accordance with plan.	B.W.

WAR DIARY
INTELLIGENCE SUMMARY

Army Form C. 2118.

Place	Date	Hour	Summary of Events and Information	Remarks and references to Appendices
YPRES SALIENT	20/9/17	5.40am	No.2 Section moved forward with Reserve Coy of 7th KLR & No.4 Section (less 1 gun in Reserve in POMMERN REDOUBT) moved forward with Reserve Coy of 9th KLR.	
"	"	—	No 2 Section's advance was delayed by Infantry being held up at IBERIAN FARM and our guns were brought into action on the left flank by the Section Sgt. T. Curryer a number of enemy returning from IBERIAN to DELVA FARM. The section officer No 2 had been wounded prior to this Sgt T. Curryer being taken command of the Section. No 4 Section (3 guns) reached its objective at GALLIPOLI HILL 35 without incident. During its advance one gun of No 2 Section was put out of action by shell fire & the remaining No 4 Section POMMERN REDOUBT was sent up to take its place and took up the required position at IRMA.	
"	"	8.35am	The 5th & 6th KLR moved forward formed the 1st objective (dotted red line). No 1 Section advanced on the Right with Reserve Coy of 5th KLR. No 3 Section with Reserve Coy of 6th KLR on the left. Had other guns come into action before reaching their objective. The remainder took up position as shown in reference to attached map :— 1 gun at about D.20.C.20.50, protecting the Div.— Right Flank & working in conjunction with the SOUTH AFRICAN BRIGADE on our right. 3 guns at about D.20.A.65.65, D.20.A.50.40, D.20.A.80.25 (No 3) D.20.A.50.40 (No 1)	map marked P.1

WAR DIARY or INTELLIGENCE SUMMARY

Army Form C. 2118.

Place	Date	Hour	Summary of Events and Information	Remarks and references to Appendices
YPRES SALIENT	20/9/17	—	No 1 firing S.E. covering the front to the Right. No 2 firing N.E. covering the front of HILL 37, and No 3 firing N.E. Two guns on the left were unable to get forward owing to troops but later moved forward into positions near GALLIPOLI COPSE and one at HILL 37. The gun at HILL 37 was immediately put out of action on arrival by shellfire. During this advance the Section Officer of No 1 Section became a casualty (wounded) & prior to this the Section left was broken also became a casualty, the command of the Section devolving upon a Cpl.	
"	"	—	During the early part of the afternoon a small local counter-attack on the Div's left was broken up by the fire from the guns on HILL 35.	
"	"	6 pm	A strong counter attack was broken up by the Lewis & M.G. Barrage, a few targets being obtained by the advanced M.G's of the Company.	
"	21/9/17	—	Nothing of importance to report	
"	22/9/17	—	During the afternoon, owing to enemy movement appearing on our left, another gun was pushed forward to GALLIPOLI COPSE to protect the left flank of the Bde & if necessary to help the gun already there to deal with any enemy attack from direction of the "SNAG". One gun was also moved forward from IRMA to a point about 200 x E of DELVA FARM to command HILL 37. The final position of the guns of the Company were from an attached map.	See map number P.1.

Army Form C. 2118.

WAR DIARY
or
INTELLIGENCE SUMMARY.
(Erase heading not required.)

Instructions regarding War Diaries and Intelligence Summaries are contained in F.S. Regs., Part II. and the Staff Manual respectively. Title pages will be prepared in manuscript.

Place	Date	Hour	Summary of Events and Information	Remarks and references to Appendices
YPRES SALIENT (POPERN REDOUBT SECTOR)	22/23 Sept (4)	—	8 Nos 1 & 2 of 174 M.G Coy were sent up to the 8 positions to get accustomed to the positions.	
"	23/24 Sept.	—	The Coys were relieved by the 174th M.G Coy who took over 8 positions. "Relief Completed at about 4.30 a.m on 24th. Relief delayed by stack ground, most of night taken by reason of the guide troops being destroyed by the heavy bombardments which had taken place. Total casualties in the action M.G.C. 3 off. Wounded. 16 O.R Killed 30 O.R wounded. Of O.Rs attached Infantry (32) were as Ammunition Carriers 3 were killed, 9 wounded & 3 missing. During the action the Allowed Forward Liquid Station & Coy H.Qrs proved invaluable both for our own use & also for the use of the Brigade H.Qrs on several occasions when all other shres were broken.	
"	24th Sept	—	Coy had finished moving from the trenches at 10.45 a.m. Proceeded during spare of afternoon to WATOU No 1 AREA where it remained for night of 24th/25th with all transport.	
WATOU No 2 AREA	25th Sept	—	Company left complete with transport & arrived at PESEL HOEK for BAPAUME at 6 p.m. train departed at 7.20 a.m.	
BAPAUME	26th Sept	—	Arrived BAPAUME at 6 a.m. Detrained & marched to camp at BARASTRE where it remained until the end of the month, refitting, reorganising etc.	
BARASTRE	30/9/17			

B. Rogers Capt
for O.C. 165th M.G Coy

16th MACHINE GUN COY.   COPY No. 11

AMENDMENT A to OPERATION ORDER No. 31

REF. MAP. FREZENBERG } 1/10,000
         GRAVENSTAFEL   18th Sept 1917.

1. Ref. Para. 3 (a)
    No. 1 SECTION will occupy positions as follows on arriving at Objective :-
        D.20.c.95.83 (STRONG POINT) firing across E. of TULIP COTTS.
        D.20.a.98.47 (TULIP COTTS.) firing NORTH.
        D.20.b.05.47 (TULIP COTTS.) firing across E. of CABBAGE COTTS
        D.20.a.90.80 (HILL 37) firing S.E. across TULIP COTTS.

    No. 2 SECTION will occupy positions as follows on arriving at Objective :-
        D.20.a.05.25 (DELTA FM) firing to protect S. flank of HILL 37 & for overhead fire on POGHT FM.
        D.20.a.05.37 (DELTA FM) firing up valley & cover Strong Point about D.20 central.
        D.19. . 53.08. (IRMA) firing N. to N.E.
        D.19.d.63.71 (KEYNORTH) firing E. along valley.

    No. 3 SECTION will occupy positions as follows on arriving at Objective :-
        D.14.c.08.15 (CAPITOL) to protect Bde Left flank
        D.14.c.09.12 (GALLIPOLI COPSE)   "   "   "   "
        D.20.b.15.85 (CABBAGE COTTS) in Strong Point firing N.
        D.20.a.66.80 (HILL 37) to cover E of Strong Point D.20.c.90.82.

    No. 4 SECTION will send 3 guns over behind 9th K.L.R. for the consolidation of the DOTTED RED LINE. The following positions will be occupied :-
        D.13.d.39.16 (GALLIPOLI) firing S.E.
        D.13.d.32.15 ("   ) firing N.E.
        D.19.b.20.76 (HILL 35) firing N. to cover left flank
    If final Objective is reached HILL 35 gun will be withdrawn, without further orders, into Reserve.
    By Brigade Orders Reserve guns are to be kept in two dugouts in DUST TRENCH. Notice Boards to be placed at ZERO on two dugouts for this purpose.

2. Ref. Para. 2 (d).
    Headquarters of Battalions at ZERO will be as follows :-
        5th K.L.R. } D.19.a.65.10
        7th K.L.R. }
        6th K.L.R. } BANK FARM
        9th K.L.R. }

   Ref. Para 2 (e)
        After "POMMERN" add "and BANK FARM."

3. Ref. Para 3
   POMMERN   No. 4 SECTION H.Q will be at DUST TRENCH in REDOUBT.

C.S.M. will have an intermediate Signal Station at or in the vicinity of JASPER and UHLAN FARMS.

Wire will be laid from WIELTJE to C.S.M. before ZERO and will be carried on to No. 4 Section in rear of 1/5th L.N. LANCS. when they move forward to POMMERN LINE at ZERO.

Copies of all verbal messages sent or received by wire to be retained.

4. Ref. Para. 9

C.S.M. will reconnoitre for and locate the Brigade Dump at C.28.d.0.1 as soon as possible after getting into position, so as to know exactly where supplies may be obtained if required.

5. GENERAL

Collect ammunition from casualties.

Use German machine guns to utmost in place of, or in addition to your own.

Very probably it will not be possible to visit gun positions by day. They must be visited by night, early morning or dusk. All men to be warned to keep concealed from view & not to give away positions by too much moving. All movement to be done by night only.

Get in touch with posts on right and left before Barrage lifts, and mark direction of N. Point by means of sticks. This should be possible as there will be a great deal of smoke in the Barrage.

Study Barrage map closely so as to know exactly when moves should take place by Time and act accordingly.

All Secret Papers & Operation Orders likely to be of use to the Enemy to be destroyed before ZERO.

COPY No. 1	O.C. No. 1 SECTION	
" 2	" 2 "	
" 3	" 3 "	
" 4	" 4 "	
" 5	2LT. HALSTEAD	
" 6	" D S. WHICHELOW	
" 7	" SOUTHALL	
" 8	C.O.	
" 9	O.C. TRANSPORT	
" 10	C.S.M.	
" 11	WAR DIARY	
" 12	FILE	

L. Parves Capt

for O.C. 165th M.G.Coy.

SECRET.

165TH MACHINE GUN COMPANY.

OPERATION ORDER No. 31.

PRELIMINARY

COPY No 11

Ref. Mp FREZENBERG 1/10000.   17th SEPT. 1917

1. (a) The V Corps is to take part in offensive operations at an early date.

   (b) The attack will be carried out by the 9th DIVISION on the Right and the 55th DIVISION on the Left. The 3rd & 59th Divisions will be in Corps Reserve.

   (c) The 58th Division (XVIII Corps) will be on the immediate Left of the 55th Division. The 28th South African Brigade will be on the right of the 55th Division.

2. (a) The attack by the 55th Division will be delivered on the front shown on the map previously issued, final objective being the GREEN LINE. 165th Bde will be on the Right and 164th Bde on the Left. One battalion of 166th Bde will be attached to each of 164th & 165th Brigades. The remaining two Battalions of 166th Brigade will be in Divisional Reserve.

   (b) 164th & 165th Brigade Headquarters at WIELTJE Dugouts.

   (c) 165th Inf. Brigade will attack the first objective with 7th K.L.R. on Right, 9th K.L.R. on Left, 5th K.L.R. in Support on the Right, 6th K.L.R. in Support on the Left.

   1/5th L.N.Lancs will be in Reserve in the old German Front Line, and will move to the STUTZPUNKT LINE at ZERO.

   After the first objective has been taken the 5th K.L.R. and 6th K.L.R. will move forward and attack the 2nd Objective.

   (d) DISPOSITIONS at ZERO 7th & 9th K.L.R. will be disposed in present front line shell holes 5th & 6th K.L.R. in the STUTZPUNKT LINE (Headquarters of all four Battalions probably – POMMERN REDOUBT.)

3. MACHINE GUNS.

   (a) The machine guns of this Company will be employed as follows:-

   No. 1 SECTION (i/c 2Lt. BROWN.) will advance with Reserve line of 5th Kings up to the 2ND Objective.

   No. 2 SECTION (i/c Lt. BRAY) will advance with Reserve Line of 7th & 9th Kings up to the 1st Objective.

-7-

NO. 3 SECTION (I/c 2LT. HALSTEAD) will advance with Rear Line of 6th Kings to the 2nd Objective.

NO. 4 SECTION (I/c LT. STRETCH) will be in Brigade Reserve and will act as a forward depot between Company H.Q (WIELTJE DUGOUTS) and the forward Sections.

(b) On arrival at their Objectives O.C's Nos. 1, 2 and 3 Sections will place their guns in positions in accordance with orders to be given later by Coy. H.Q. They will then come under the Tactical Command of O.C. the Battn. in the Sector in which the guns are.

Guns will not be at the disposal of Company or Platoon Commanders. O.C. Sections will therefore keep in close touch with their respective Bn. HQ's.

4. FORMATION -

Each Battalion will attack in four waves with 50 yards distance between waves.

5. OBJECTIVES.

(a) For the 7th & 9th K.L.R (First Objective) will be the RED DOTTED LINE and the YELLOW LINE. Bn. HQ's will remain at POMMERN

For the 5th & 6th K.L.R. (2nd Objective) will be the GREEN LINE. 5th Bn. H.Q will be established at DELVA FARM, and of the 6th K.L.R at GALLIPOLI.

(b) 5th K.L.R & 6th K.L.R will leave the STUTZPUNKT Line in time to pass through the YELLOW LINE at Zero plus 2 hours 45 minutes (approx.). Times will be definitely fixed when the Artillery Barrage has been finally decided upon.

(c) 1/5 L.N. Lancs will move to the STUTZPUNKT LINE at ZERO, and will move to a line DELVA GALLIPOLI at ZERO plus 2 hours 45 minutes

6. ENEMY STRONG POINTS

Definite parties of at least a Platoon in strength will be told off for the attack and garrison of the following points by the Battalion in whose area they are situated :-

GALLIPOLI, HILL 35 (LENS), IBERIAN, DELVA, CAPITOL HILL 37.

7 BARRAGE.

The attack will be carried out under a creeping Barrage, combined with a Machine Gun Barrage, and a heavy bombardment of all known Strong Points & Communications. The Barrage (as at present arranged) will open 150 yards in front of the

Infantry and will move forward by leaps of 50 yards, first lift at ZERO plus 3 minutes. For the first 200 yards it will move at the rate of 100 yards in 4 minutes, then at 100 yds in 6 minutes. When the protective Barrage lifts from 150 yards beyond the RED DOTTED LINE, the pace of the Barrage will be at 100 yards in 8 minutes with a pause of 40 minutes 150 yards beyond the YELLOW LINE.

8. COMMUNICATIONS.

(a) A Company Signal Station will if possible be established at HQrs of O.C. No. 4 Section connected by wire with Coy. HQrs (WIELTJE DUGOUTS).

(b) One runner from each Section to be left at Coy. H.Q. to be employed as in the previous operations on 31st July.

(c) Brigade wires will also be run to HILL 35 and later to HILL 37.

(d) Messages sent by Brigade Wire should also be duplicated by runner to Coy. Station at No. 4 Section HQ.

(e) Messages from No. 1 Section to be signed as from "O.C. Right Forward Section", from No. 2 Section as from "O.C. Yellow Section", from No. 3 Section as from "O.C. Left Forward Section", and from No. 4 Section as from "O.C. Reserve Section".

9. SUPPLIES, DUMPS, S.A.A.

Brigade Dump near No. 5 Track, about C.23.d.0.1 containing 100,000 S.A.A., Water tins 600 etc.

Forward Dumps at BANK FARM and POMMERN REDOUBT containing each 50000 S.A.A., Water tins 100, etc. From these Forward Dumps the Coy can draw up to 25 tins water, if required.

10. PACK MULES.

If required for formation of forward S.A.A. Dumps will be under the command 2/Lt. A.S. WHICHELOW, to whom detailed orders will be given later.

COPY No. 1 — O.C. No. 1 SECTION
" 2 — " 2 "
" 3 — " 3 "
" 4 — " 4 "
" 5 — 2 LT. HALSTEAD
" 6 — 2 LT. A.S. WHICHELOW
" 7 — 2 LT. SOUTHALL
" 8 — C.O.
" 9 — O.C. TRANSPORT
" 10 — C.S.M.
" 11 — WAR DIARY
" 12 — FILE

H Ramsley
for O.C. 165th M.G.Coy.

165th Machine Gun Company
Operation Order No. 30.

Ref Maps. Sheet 28 N.W. Edition 6A 1/20000
Hazebrouck 5A

Copy No. 11
Sept 13th 1917

1. 163rd Machine Gun Company will move to the forward area on the 14th and 15th Sept. in accordance with the following orders.

2. TRANSPORT - less 8 G.S. limbers, Water Cart and Officers' Mess Cart - will move under B.T.O. on the 14th inst to WORMHOUDT "A" Area.
Starting point - Road junction immediately S of second L in BAYENGHEM-LEZ-EPERLEQUES. Time 9.10 am. On the 15th inst the move will be continued at 6 am. to VLAMERTINGHE No. 2 Area.

3. BILLETING PARTY. 2Lt. J. BROWN with servant, 1 N.C.O from No. 1 Section, and 1 N.C.O. from Transport will report to Capt. R. CHARNOCK M.C at AUDRUICQ Station at 10 am. on 14th inst Party will proceed by train at 10.45 am under orders of Capt CHARNOCK.

4. Remainder of COMPANY, with 8 Fighting limbers, Water Cart, and Officers' Mess Cart will proceed by No. 4 train at 1.45 pm. on the 15th inst. from AUDRUICQ STATION to PESELHOEK. Entraining commences at 10.45 am.

5. LT. RAMAGE is detailed as Entraining Officer and will be at the Station at 10.30 am. and will report Entraining Strength of Units travelling by the train to the R.T.O.

6. LOADING PARTY. Lt. STRETCH and a party of 100 men will report to R.T.O at 10.45 am. for the purpose of loading the Train. On arrival at destination the same party will unload the train.

7. SUPPLIES.
14th Sept. Two days supplies will be issued as follows:-
Rations for consumption on 15th for personnel & Transport proceeding by rail will be delivered direct to Units by Lorry. For personnel proceeding by road rations for consumption on 15th inst. will be delivered at Staging Area WORMHOUDT in the afternoon, together with Rations for the whole Company for consumption on the 16th inst.
16th Sept Refilling Point at G.H.d. at 10 am.

8. ORDNANCE.
Refilling point closes at NORDAUSQUES on 13th & opens at POPERINGHE on 15th.

9. POST.
During the move mails will be delivered at Supply Refilling Points.

F. Parsons Capt

for O.C. 165TH MACHINE GUN COY.

Copy No. 1. — O.C. No. 1 Section
" No. 2 — " " 2 "
" No. 3 — " " 3 "
" No. 4 — " " 4 "
" No. 5 — " Transport
" No. 6 — 2 LT. Halstead
" No. 7 — 2 LT Whichelow
" No. 8 — 2 LT Southall
" No. 9 — C.S.M.
" No. 10 — C.Q.M.S.
" No. 11 — War Diary
" No. 12 — File

CONFIDENTIAL

W.D. 21

War Diary
of
165th M.G. Coy
for the period
1st to 31st October, 1917

185h
M/G. Coy

WAR DIARY
or
INTELLIGENCE SUMMARY.
(Erase heading not required.)

Army Form C. 2118.

Place	Date	Hour	Summary of Events and Information	Remarks and references to Appendices
BARASTRE	1/10/17	9.45am 2.30pm	Company worked, completed work mounted portion. to AIZECOURT-LE-BAS. Arrived at 8.30 pm	OO No 32 attached
AIZECOURT	2/10/17	2.25pm	Left AIZECOURT-LE-BAS for trenches to relieve 106 M.G.Coy in Right Brigade Sector.	
STE EMILIE	"	4.30pm	Arrived at 106 M.G.Coy HQrs. Relief commenced at about 7.15 p.m. Complete by 10 p.m. No trouble attended the relief. 12 guns in position in the trenches, 4 guns in Reserve at Coy HQrs	
"	3/10/17		Usual trench Routine. Interior Economy carried out at nights. Aeroplanes engaged when provided by M.G. Fire	
"	8/10/17		General improvement of accommodation, dug outs etc	
"	"		Operation Order No 33 issued for Concentration Shoot with 10 guns in cooperation with Artillery & T.M's Very feeble enemy retaliation.	OO 33 attached
"	9/10/17		Concentration Shoot duly carried out - apparently with success. Very feeble enemy retaliation.	
"	10/10/17		Usual trench routine	
"	4/10/17		Operation Order No. 34, in reference to relief by 164 M.G.Coy taking over of Left Brigade Sector from 156 M.G.Coy	OO.34 attached
"	4/10/17	6 p.m.	164 M.G.Coy commenced to relief commenced. Weather very bad - very dark & pouring with rain. During relief enemy shelled tracks & roads to some extent hampered the relief. Apparently he expected a relief that night probably from information obtained from two prisoners taken by us captured from 186th Batn in the previous night. No casualties resulted to this Company. Relief complete - Right Sector at about midnight.	
EPEHY SECTOR	17/10/17	1.45am	Relief complete - Left Brigade Sector	
"	12/10/17		Usual trench routine, 12 guns in position, 4 in Reserve at Coy HQrs	

A.P.Parsons Capt.
115 M.G.Coy.

165th.
M.G. Coy

WAR DIARY
INTELLIGENCE SUMMARY.
(Erase heading not required.)

Army Form C. 2118.

Place	Date	Hour	Summary of Events and Information	Remarks and references to Appendices
EPEHY SECTOR	14/10/17 to 16/10/17		Usual trench routine. Activity normal, ie very quiet	
	17/10/17	10pm	Concentration shoot by 8 machine guns in conjunction with attacking 3 T.M.s on HONNECOURT WOOD	
			Nothing unusual attended the operation - no enemy retaliation - results of shoot reported satisfactory	
	18/10/17 to 21/10/17		Usual trench routine. Activity normal.	
"	22/10/17	6.20am	A small operation carried out by 8 m.guns in conjunction with 165 T.M.B. & c. A barrage was put up across OSSUS WOOD to cover 4 Stokes Mortars which went out into NO MAN'S LAND to fire a hurricane bombardment at certain points where it had been reported that enemy movement was observed in early mornings. Shoot appears successful & T.M.s & enemy infantry withdrew without cessation after the operation had been completed.	
"	23/10/17		Relieved by 164 M.G. Coy as per Operation Order No 35. Relief complete by 10 p.m. after relief Company marched independently by Sections to AIZECOURT-LE-BAS	OO 35 attached
AIZECOURT-LE-BAS	23/10/17 to 31/10/17		Company in camp under Canvas. Usual daily training & drill Operation Order No 36 re relief of 164 M.G.Coy in Right Reserve Sector issued on 31/10/17	OO 36 attached

W. Rawson Capt
for OC 165th Machine Gun Coy

SECRET

163rd MACHINE GUN Coy.

OPERATION ORDER No 36   COPY No 9

REF. TRENCH MAPS. and
1/20000 62 c. N.E.   31st Oct 1917

1. This Company will relieve the 164th M.G. Coy in the Right Brigade Sector on the night 1st/2nd Nov.

2. DISPOSITIONS. — Sectors will be relieved as follows:—

    | No. 1 SECTION. | RIGHT SECTOR (BOIS! BOULOGNE) | CAT POST
R.6
DUNCAN POST
BROCK (F.10.d.1Y.12) |

    | No. 2 SECTION. (plus 1 gun No. 3 Section.) | CENTRE SECTOR (TOMBOIS FARM) | EGO POST
FLEECEALL POST
R 14 } GRAFTON POST
R 15 }
ISLAND TRAVERSE (F.3 a) |

    | No. 3. SECTION less 1 gun. | LEFT SECTOR (LEMPIRE ROAD) | F 5   EAGLE'S NEST
R.17 CRUCIFORM T.
R.18 MALASSISE FM |

    No. 4 SECTION   In reserve at St. EMILIE.

3. GUIDES. Guides for each gun team will be at Section H.Q. at 3.30 pm.

4. TAKING OVER. Belt Boxes, in addition to the usual trench stores, will be taken over. Lists of trench stores taken over to be forwarded to Orderly Room by 8 am. on the 2nd. Nov.

    Indirect fire position and programmes to be taken over and Indirect fire to be carried on as programme. Records of firing up to time of relief are also to be taken over.

5. TRANSPORT. Animals for the 5 gun limbers at present camp to be at Coy. HQrs by 9.30 am.

    Three limbers and mess cart for Coy. HQrs baggage to be at Coy. HQrs at 8.30 am.

    Water cart to be removed from Camp at 10 am. and left at ST. EMILIE by 4 pm.

    Officers' mounts to be at Camp at 9.45 am.

6. WATER & RATIONS. The same arrangements for water supply as when last in Right Brigade Sector.

-2-

Rations for the 2nd. hour to be delivered as usual to Section and Coy. HQrs in the line as per para. 2.

7. Relief complete to be notified to Coy. HQrs St. EMILIE without delay.
  Code word "RIGHT".

COPIES
  No. 1 — O.C. No. 1 Section
  " 2 — "   " 2   "
  " 3 — "   " 3   "
  " 4 — "   " 4   "
  " 5 — O.C. Transport
  " 6 — C.Q.M.S.
  " 7 — C.S.M.
  " 8 — File
  " 9 }
  " 10 } War Diary

F.F. Parsons Capt.
O.C. 165th M.G.Coy.

SECRET

165th Machine Gun Company
OPERATION ORDER No 35   Copy No 7

Ref. Trench Maps
62c.N.E. 1/20000   21st October 1917

1. This Company will be relieved by the 166th Machine Gun Coy on the night 22/23rd October, and after relief will proceed independently by Sections to Camp at AIZECOURT-LE-BAS.

2. **HANDING OVER.** Belt boxes in addition to the usual trench stores will be handed over and receipts obtained. Receipts to be forwarded to Orderly Room by 9.30 a.m. on the 23rd October.
Indirect Fire Positions and Targets, records of firing up to the time of relief; Log Books and all maps handed over when the Company came into the Sector are also to be handed over.
Petrol tins belonging to Sections will not be handed over.

3. **GUIDES.** If any guides are required arrangements will be notified later.

4. **TRANSPORT.** So far as is known at present the Transport of 166th M.G.Coy only will be used for the relief, one limber being provided per Section. These limbers are to be unloaded immediately on arrival at Camp and returned without delay to 166th M.G.Coy Transport Lines.

5. An Advance Party of 1 Officer (Lt. T.N.H. STRETCH) and 1 N.C.O and man from No 4 Section will proceed to AIZECOURT-LE-BAS at 1 pm to take over the Camp from 166th M.G.Coy, and arrange for accommodation of each Section on arrival.

6. Relief complete will be notified to Coy. HQ. by runner, or personally by Section Officers, code word "CAMP."

Copy No.1 - OC. No.1 Section
      2 - "   No.2   "
      3 - "   No.3   "
      4 - "   No.4   "
      5 - C.Q.M.S.
      6 - FILE
      7 } WAR DIARY
      8 }

C. Parsons Capt
O.C. 165th M.G.Coy

165TH MACHINE GUN COY

Amendment 'A' to OPERATION ORDER No. 34

As the 164th M.G.Coy may be unable to arrive at St. EMILIE until 6.30 pm. all the times stated will be one hour later for guides and transport.

11/10/17

E Parnos Capt
for O.C. 165 M G Coy

SECRET   COPY No 8

165TH MACHINE GUN COMPANY

OPERATION ORDER No. 34.

Ref. Trench Maps 57c.SE }
                  62c.NE } 1/20000
Gillemont Farm 1/10000
Sketch Map W.L 77 1/20000 (already issued)

11th October 1917

1. On the night 12/13th October the 165th Machine Gun Coy will be relieved in the Right Brigade Sector by the 164th M.G. Coy, and after relief will relieve the 166th M.G.Coy in the Left Brigade Sector.

2. **GUIDES FOR 164TH M.G.Coy** - One guide per Section will report at Coy. HQrs at 5 pm. to guide relieving Sections to Section H.Qrs. These guides will bring back to Coy. HQrs the bicycles, if any, at present in possession of their Sections.

3. **HANDING OVER** - All belt boxes in addition to the usual trench stores are to be handed over and receipts obtained. Maps (1/10000) and Indirect Fire Positions and Targets are to be handed over, together with records of Indirect Firing up to time of relief.
   All Water tins which are the property of this Company and all A.A. M.G sights are to be taken by Sections to their new Sectors.

4. **RELIEF COMPLETE** in the Right Brigade Sector will be notified to present Coy. HQrs by the Code word "PLANT" sent by Runner of relieving Section. Section Runners will accompany their Sections to the new Sector immediately after relief.

5. After relief Sections will proceed independently to their Sectors, as already allotted, in the Left Brigade Sector and will carry out relief without delay.

6. **GUIDES** for **LEFT BDE SECTOR**. As already arranged between O.C's Sections concerned.
   1 guide for No. 3 Section at FALLEN TREE RD JUNCTION, F.1.b.85.75 at 5.30 p.m. for Left forward Section HQrs.
   1 guide for No. 1 Section will be at FALLEN TREE ROAD JUNCTION, F.1.b.85.75 at 7.45 p.m. for LIMERICK POST

-2-

GUIDES for No. 2 SECTION at 8 p.m. at Right Forward Section HQrs for Positions :- F5, F6, F7 & F8.

GUIDES for No. 4 SECTION at 8 p.m. at Rear Section HQrs for positions :- R.20, R.21, R.22 & R.24.

7. TAKING OVER. Belt boxes will be taken over in addition to the usual trench stores; receipts being given. Copies of Receipts to be forwarded to Coy. HQ. by 8 a.m. on the 13th Oct. All Indirect Fire Positions and Targets will be taken over together with records of firing up to time of relief. Arrangements are to be made to carry on with the Indirect Fire Programme for the night and complete Indirect Fire Reports for 24 hours preceding 7.30 a.m. on 13th Oct. will be forwarded to Coy HQ at the usual time.

8. RELIEF COMPLETE in Left Bde Sector will be notified to Coy H.Q (PARRS BANK) by Runners - Code Word "PARROT"

9. TRANSPORT. Transport for relief will be required as follows :-

No. 3 SECTION - 1 Limber to report at Coy. HQ at 4.45 p.m.
No. 1 " - 1 " " " at Section HQ at 7 p.m.
Remaining Sections 2 limbers each, to report at Section HQrs at 7 p.m.
H.Q. - 2 limbers & mess cart to report at Coy HQ at 4.45p
Water Cart will be removed from ST. EMILIE to Transport lines at 7 p.m.

10. WATER SUPPLY - In the Left Brigade Sector any Water tins which cannot be filled from wells in the line are to be returned nightly to Coy. HQrs for filling. Transport will call each night for the filled tins.

COPY No.1 - O.C. No.1 SECTION
"   2   "   " 2   "
"   3   "   " 3   "
"   4   "   " 4   "
"   5   O.C. 164TH M.G.COY
"   6   "   166   "
"   7   FILE
"   8   { WAR DIARY

H Parrs Capt.
for O.C. 165TH MACHINE GUN COY

SECRET

165th MACHINE GUN COMPANY

COPY No. 3

OPERATION ORDER No. 33

REFERENCE TRENCH MAP 1/10000
62 B. N.W)
62. C.) 1/20000

8th October 1917

1. On the 9th October 10 Machine Guns of 165th, 166 & 164th Machine Gun Companies will carry out M.G Fire in conjunction with Artillery and Trench Mortars in accordance with the following orders:-

2. RIGHT GROUP - 4 guns under Command of LT. McLELLAN (165 M.G Co)
   LEFT GROUP - 6 guns under Command of LT. STURGE (196 M.G Co)

3. Details of Gun positions, Targets and Fire Orders as per attached Programme.

4. Rate of Fire - One belt in 2 minutes.

5. SYNCHRONIZATION. OC Groups will synchronise watches at 2.30 pm at No. 2 Section (165 M.G Co) H.Qrs at F.16.c.12.55. To which it will be sent by Runner from 165th M.G Coy H.Qrs.

6. ZERO HOUR will be at 4 pm.

COPY No. 1 - OC RIGHT GROUP
       2 - " LEFT "
       3 - WAR DIARY
       4 - FILE
       5 - SPARE

S.R Parsons Capt
for OC. 165th M.G Co.

FIRE PROGRAMME ACCOMPANYING 165th MACHINE GUN Co's OPERATION ORDER No. 33

8-10-17

GROUP	POSITION	TIME OF FIRE	TARGET	DIRECTION (MAGNETIC)		DESCRIPTION OF FIRE	RANGE (YARDS)	Q.E.	REMARKS
RIGHT	Along Hussar Road at 20ft intervals Left gun at F.23.c.00.75	Zero to Zero + 10 mins	Area including B.13.a.90.00 A.14.a.15.40	No.1 Gun (RIGHT GUN) " 2 " 3 " 4 (LEFT GUN)	72°48' 70°48' 69°18' 68°48'	Vertical Searching – " – – " – – " –	2250ˣ - 2500 2500 - 2250 2250ˣ - 2500 2500 - 2250	5°41' to 7°28' 7°28' to 5°41' 5°41' to 7°28' 7°28' to 5°41'	Target and gun level
LEFT	Along Ken Lane at 20ft intervals Left gun at F.14.a.10.60	Zero to Zero + 10 mins	Area including A.14.c.50.77 A.14.a.60.12	No.1 Gun (RIGHT GUN) 2 3 4 5 6 (LEFT GUN)	110°48' 111°18' 109°18' 109°48' 109°46' 108°15'	Each gun Traversing 1° RIGHT and 1° LEFT of Zero Line	2145ˣ 2025 2145ˣ 2025 2145ˣ 2025	4°38' 3°41' 4°38' 3°41' 4°38' 3°41'	Target 20 metres below gun

165TH MACHINE GUN COY

OPERATION ORDER No. 32.   COPY No. 8

REF MAPS:-
TRENCH MAP 62C. N.E. 1/10000
PAPER MAP - W.L. 76a. 1/20000 (already issued)

1st October 1917

1. On the evening 2nd/3rd October the 165th Machine Gun Company will relieve the 106th Machine Gun Coy in the Right Brigade Sector.

2. **DISPOSITION OF GUNS**.
   (a) No. 1 Section will take over the "Front Positions" comprising the following:-
      (1) FLEECEALL POST.
      (2) EGG POST
      (3) DULEFUL POST
      (4) DUNCAN POST

   (b) No. 2 Section will take over the "Right Support Positions" comprising the following:-
      (1) CAT POST
      (2) BASSE BOULOGNE SOUTH (2 guns)
      (3) LEMPIRE CENTRAL.

   (c) No. 4 Section will take over the "Left Support Positions" comprising the following:-
      (1) GRAFTON POST. (2 guns).
      (2) BROCK
      (3) "A" GROUP.

   (d) No. 3 Section will be in reserve at COY H.Q.

3. **GUIDES**. Relief will commence at 7.30 p.m. from Coy Hqrs at ST. EMILIE, guides being provided as follows:-

   To (a) (1) & (2) — 1 guide } No. 1 Section
   " (a) (3) & (4) — 1   "   }
   " (b) 1, 2 & 3 — 1   "   " 2 Section
   " (c) 1, 2 & 3 — 1   "   " 4 Section

4. **TAKING OVER**. Belt boxes will not be taken over. All other Trench Stores are to be taken over and receipts given. Lists of Trench Stores taken over to be rendered to Orderly Room by 8 am on 3rd inst.

5. **SIGNALS**. Signal Corporal will take over from 106th M.G.Coy all Telephone wires belonging to the Coy and will obtain full particulars and instructions in regard to same.

6. **TRANSPORT**. The following Transport will be required for the relief:-

- 2 -

　　For (a), (1) and (2) — 1 Limber } No. 1 Section
　　For (a), (3) " (4) — 1 Limber }

　　For (b), (1) and (2) — 1 Limber } No. 2 Section
　　For (b) (3) — 1 Limber }

　　For (c), (1) — 1 Limber } No. 4 Section
　　For (c), (2) and (3) — 1 Limber }

　　For Coy. H.Q. — 1 Limber, 1 mess cart and water cart.

　　For No. 3 Section — 1 Limber.

　　The above Transport will be packed tomorrow morning and will be brought up by Transport Officer so as to arrive at Coy. HQ. ST. EMILIE at 7.15 p.m.

　　At 2 pm. 1 Limber containing Cook's gear, and as much HQrs Stores as possible will proceed to ST. EMILIE accompanied by 2 Cooks, Signal Corporal and Coy. Artificer.

7. **PACKING OF LIMBERS.** Limbers will be packed with all necessary gun gear and equipment, used 8 Belt boxes only per gun will be packed; the balance being left in the limbers in care of T.O. One spare barrel only to be taken into the line per Section; this will be kept at Section H.Q. Spare parts Boxes and 3 spare barrels per Section will be handed over to Coy. Artificer during the morning and packed in one of H.Q limbers. First Aid Cases only will be taken into the line with the guns.

8. **WATER.** Nos. 1, 2 & 4 Sections will each pack 10 Water tins (filled) on its limbers. These will be at the rate of 2 per Team and 2 per Section H.Q. Five fresh tins of water will be brought up each night and five empty tins must be returned from each Section every night. These Water Tins are the property of the Company and are not to be treated as Trench Stores, but are to be brought out on relief.
　　The Water Cart will be used to supply Coy. HQ and the Reserve Section with water.

9. 　　One bicycle will be at the disposal of O.C. No. 4 Section for use of Section Runner.

10. 　　The Company will proceed by Route March to ST. EMILIE. Time of arrival 4.15 pm. Tea on arrival.

11. Completion of Relief will be reported to Bgé. H.Q. as early as possible, by Runner, or by wire to "HG" code word "POOL".

COPY. No. 1.   OC. No. 1 SECTION
  "   2   "   2   "
  "   3   "   3   "
  "   4   "   4   "
  "   5   "   TRANSPORT
  "   6   C.S.M.
  "   7   FILE
  "   8   WAR DIARY
  "   9   SPARE

L. S. Parsons, Capt.

for OC. 165th Machine Gun Cy

War Diary
of the
16th to 1st Coy
Post Motherover
1st to 30th November
1917

165/55 W/22

186th M.G. Coy.
WAR DIARY
or
INTELLIGENCE SUMMARY.
(Erase heading not required.)

Army Form C. 2118.

Instructions regarding War Diaries and Intelligence Summaries are contained in F. S. Regs., Part II. and the Staff Manual respectively. Title pages will be prepared in manuscript.

Place	Date	Hour	Summary of Events and Information	Remarks and references to Appendices
STE EMILIE SOMME	1/11/17	9.45 pm	Company left AIZECOURT-LE-BAS and proceeded by route march to STE EMILIE to relieve 143rd M.G. Coy in the Right Brigade Sector. Nos 1, 2 & 3 Sections	ASI
SHEET 62cNE	2.45 am		moved to the trenches at 3.45 pm. No 4 Section remained in Reserve at	
			Coy HQrs. Relief completed without by section by 5 pm.	
	2/11/17 - 3/11/17		Enemy artillery quite. Usual indirect fire carried out	
	4/11/17	4 am	Enemy bombarded our front line for 20 minutes. Damage slight to newly	
			repaired trenches at DUNCAN and CAT POSTS. Enemy subsequently raided	
			DOG TR capturing 2 men	
	5/11/17		Situation normal. Usual indirect fire carried out	
	6/11/17	2.30 am	Concentration shoot on Enemy trenches on AY and A8	
			No 3 Section had one casualty	
	7/11/17		Enemy artillery active. Weather dull and raining. DUNCAN and CAT	
	8/11/17		POSTS bombarded	
	9/11/17		MG Barrage positions reconnoitred for forthcoming operations	
	10/11/17 - 11/11/17		Usual indirect firing. Work on MG Barrage positions. Shelters	
			formation of SAA dumps for the MG Batterys	ASI

A6945   Wt. W1442/M160   350,000   12/16   D. D. & L.   Forms/C/2118/44

105th M.G. Coy.
WAR DIARY
or
INTELLIGENCE SUMMARY.

Place	Date	Hour	Summary of Events and Information	Remarks and references to Appendices
	16/11/17		Relieved by 164th M.G.Coy. Nos 1, 2 & 3 Sections each left a working party of 1 Officer N.C.O. & 8 men to continue work on shelters at the M.G. Barrage positions. Remainder of Company after relief moved to billets at VILLERS FAUCON	Nothing
	17/11/17		Baths and general cleaning up of guns equipment etc	
	19/11/17	2:30 pm	Company moved off from VILLERS FAUCON for ST EMILIE, where they had Tea	
		3 pm	Officers conference at M.G.Coy HQ STE EMILIE	
		5:30 pm	Sections moved off for to their respective assembly positions	
			No.1 Section to HUSSAR ROAD (F.22.d.9.8) No.2 Section to PANTPANUS LANE No.3 Section to KEN LANE No.4 Section to HUSSAR RD	
			Our artillery active at intervals during night	
	19/11/17		The day being Y day it was spent in preparing for the operations on Z day	
		5 pm	Major Jayne DSO of now in command HQrs at E.16.c.35.65	
	20/11/17	6 am	Synchronised time was sent to Sections from Adv HQrs	
			Enemy shelled FREECEAL and POPPAEUS LANES at 4 am, 5 am & 5:30 am	
		6:10 am	Enemy opened fire for 10 minutes along the slopes behind TOMBUIS Fm & ICELEW POST	

WAR DIARY or INTELLIGENCE SUMMARY

186th M.G. Coy.

Army Form C. 2118.

- 3 -

Place	Date	Hour	Summary of Events and Information	Remarks and references to Appendices
	20/11/17	6.20am ZERO HOUR	The 11th Inf. Bde. attacked GOLEMONT FARM at ZERO + 3 and the Knoll at ZERO plus 30. The 9th KLR of 165th Inf. Bde. carried out a diversionary attack South of the BIRDCAGE near OLDHAM STREET. The advance of the Infantry was covered by indirect machine gun barrage of 40 guns, of which number the C.O. of this Company had 20 under his command. Artillery opened out 15 seconds before ZERO.	
		7.35am	S.O.S. was sent up on extreme left and machine guns opened fire on their S.O.S. targets. The Infantry withdrew to their original line during the morning.	
		4.30pm	Artillery barrage opened and machine guns fired rapid fire at 4.35pm. Slow rate of fire was continued until 5.30pm.	
	Night of 20/21st		Passed very quietly	
	20/11/17	6pm	All Company guns withdrew with the exception of 2 guns of No.1 Section which rejoined 164 Bty H.Q. Company moved to billets at VILLERS FAUCON	
	22/11/17		Received Lieutenant Quin & detachment etc.	

WAR DIARY or INTELLIGENCE SUMMARY

135th M.G. Coy

Army Form C. 2118.

Place	Date	Hour	Summary of Events and Information	Remarks and references to Appendices
	23/11/17	8:45 am	Company went to Baths	
		2:30 pm	Moved to STE EMILIE to relieve the 164th Coy/M.G on the Right Brigade Sector	
		4:30 pm	Sections held up at entrance to RONSSOY by hostile shelling 20 casualties	
	24/11/17		Day & night quiet. Usual indirect fire programme carried out	
	25/11/17 - 27/11/17		Situation Quiet	
	28/11/17		Enemy aeroplanes very active flying low over our trenches	
	29/11/17	8am	Weather fine but dull. Two enemy 'planes flew over lines returning to the German lines in a northerly direction. Our artillery active during night	
	30/11/17	7:10am	S.O.S. went up over the Knoll. Our Artillery and machine guns opened fire on S.O.S lines. Enemy shelling very heavy on batteries in BASSE BOULOGNE area. Owing to a large number of gas shells used the guns teams had to wear their Box Resp. The enemy attack and advanced across the left of the Brigade Sector capturing trenches in the vicinity of BIRDCAGE and Francho to the further north. The gun & gun team at F.5 (EAGLE QUARRY) reported missing believed prisoners. Other casualties 10R. Killed and 10R Wounded	

30/11/17

W.S.[signature]
OC 165th M.G. Coy.

165 M G Coy
55 / 23

War Diary
of the
165th Infantry Brigade
for the period
1st to 31st December, 1917.

WAR DIARY
INTELLIGENCE SUMMARY

Army Form C. 2118.

Place	Date	Hour	Summary of Events and Information	Remarks and references to Appendices
SOMME STE EMILIE SECTOR	Dec 1st	10 a.m.	A Regiment of Cavalry charged past LIMERICK & KILDARE POSTS and occupied position in KILDARE LANE.	
"	"	noon	An enemy attack on the cavalry from KILDARE POST broke up one of our C/S m.g.s at CRUCIFORM POST. Fire at dusk.	
		4pm	Another attack similar to above from STONE LANE broke up in a similar manner.	
			During afternoon enemy came out of KILDARE POST apparently with object of meeting the march of the 166th of Bde. They were engaged by 2 guns of our Left Section.	
		11am	Section officer of Left Section went across to enquire to get in touch with them as operation of m.g.s with them. Proved better, their supporting objective seemed to be very uncertain. Cavalry withdrew after dusk, but on suggestion of our Section officer left two m.g.s to assist in defence of Left Flank of Brigade. Throughout the afternoon numerous targets of small parties of enemy were engaged by the guns of our Left Section. These parties were mostly carrying parties.	
		3pm	Heaviest barrage put down on CATELET COPSE & CRUCIFORM POST. Our S.O.S. sent up but our artillery did not appear to reply, no enemy guns only opening fire. Heavy shelling over whole Bde area largely with gas shells.	
	1/2/		Night passed quietly, the indirect fire being carried out by one machine gun as usual.	
	2nd De		Situation generally quiet. A lot of both sides active throughout day, gas shells being freely used by enemy (strong winds in trenches from LEMAIRE & RONSSOY. Evidently intended in harassing fire on communications.	
	3rd Dec		Situation quiet — intermittent enemy shelling — no infantry action	

GP

Army Form C. 2118.

WAR DIARY
or
INTELLIGENCE SUMMARY.
(Erase heading not required.)

Instructions regarding War Diaries and Intelligence Summaries are contained in F. S. Regs., Part II, and the Staff Manual respectively. Title pages will be prepared in manuscript.

Place	Date	Hour	Summary of Events and Information	Remarks and references to Appendices
SOMME	4th Dec	—	Situation generally quiet. Artillery actively mostly counter battery work & registration.	Enemy aerial aft flank 15.80 Coy between
STE EMILIE SECTOR	5th Dec	—	Situation quiet. Company relieved by the 48th M.G. Coy after 0.07 to 40. Relief complete at about 10 p.m. Section after relief returned to Coy H.Q. for the night at STE EMILIE	10.40 detailed Four 164 M.G. Coy guns posts
"	6th Dec	—	One Section sent up into BROWN LINE at 5.30 a.m. as Reserve for emergency. Posts to be developed & guns are watchmen at 9.30 a.m.	
"	6/12/17	12 noon	Company moved by Lorries to PERONNE. Transport left by road at about the same time	
PERONNE	"	4 pm	Arrived at PERONNE. Sent into billets at about 4 pm	
"	7/12/17	—	Cleaning up & re-organisation	
"	8/12/17	9.30 am	Company entrained at PERONNE. Transport moved off by road	
MOREUIL	"	6 pm	Company arrived at MOREUIL. Sent into huts.	
"	9/12/17	—	Cleaning up & re-organisation. Camp bombed on the night of = 10th - probably - mistaken for aerodrome close by.	
"	11/12/17	—		
"	12/12/17	—	Company proceeded by march route complete with mounted personnel & transport to BETHENCOURT	
—	13/12/17	—	- do - do - to BRIAS. Billeta at LE GROSSART.	
—	14/12/17	—	" " to LISBOURG	
LISBOURG	15/12/17 to 31/1/17	—	Re-organisation, refitting and training. Handicapped by severe frosts & snow	

H Beam. Cpt.
165 OT M.G. Coy

4. OC Most Section will hand over the Signal Station at ABARSOISE RED FARM. The instrument will not be handed over.

5. After Relay Stations will proceed to Coy HQrs STE EMILIE where they will be billeted for the night.

6. TRANSPORT. One limber per section will be sent to each Section HQrs to bring out guns, equipment &c. These limbers will be left at Coy HQrs after firing.

E.W. ross. Capt
2/o O.C. 160 NGCoy.

SECRET

165th Machine Gun Company
OPERATION ORDER No. 40.

REF. TRENCH MAPS.   5th DECR. 1917

1. This company will be relieved in the line tonight (5th/6th) by the 48th M.G. Coy.

2. Relieving sections will leave Coy HQrs at 5.30 pm. to relieve Sections as follows:—

No. 1 Section — (2Lt. WHICHELLW) — 4 positions MALASSISE FM
No. 2 "   (Lt. M°LELLAN) — 3 "   { PRIEL CUTTING
                                       { CRUCIFORM
                                       { GRAFTON Rd

No. 4 "   (2Lt. SOUTHALL) — 4 " { GRAFTON ?
                                       { FLEECEALL
                                       { EGG
                                       { ISLAND TRAVERSE

No. 3 "   (Lt. BEAUCHAMP) — 4 " { CAT POST
                                       { DUNCAN POST
                                       { BASSE BOULOGNE
                                                   (R)

3. HANDING OVER. All Belt boxes and the usual trench stores will be handed over, the usual receipts being obtained. Water Tins will not be handed over. All maps & Indirect Fire Schemes are to be handed over, and Officers are responsible that relieving Officers are informed of the exact arcs of their guns

165th MACHINE GUN COY.
OPERATION ORDER No. 39

REF. MAP 62 c. N.E. 1/10000 and
SPECIAL MAPS

COPY No. 8

18th NOVEMBER 1917.

---

1. **ATTACK.** An attack will be carried out on 'Z' day by 164 Infantry Brigade against the portion of the enemy's front trench from A.13.d.3.8. on the South to F.6.a.5.7 on the North.

    Direct attacks will be delivered on GILLEMONT FARM at ZERO plus 3 minutes and the KNOLL at ZERO plus 30 mins.

    The remainder of the front line will be captured by means of bombing attacks.

    The advance of the assaulting battalions will be regulated by the lifts of barrages as detailed in the map to be issued later.

    GILLEMONT FARM ATTACK.

    The assaulting infantry of the 1/4th R. LANCS. opposite this section of line will not leave their trenches until ZERO plus 2 minutes.

    KNOLL ATTACK.

    1/8th. L'POOL and 2/5th. L.F. will leave their trenches at ZERO plus 24 minutes and close up to the artillery barrage.

2. **GAS.** If the wind is favourable there will be a discharge of Gas.

3. **COMMUNICATION TRENCH.** A communication trench will be dug by the Pioneers from LARK POST to F.6.a.5.7.

4. **SMOKE and THERMIT.** With the object of preventing enemy observation whilst our infantry are advancing on the KNOLL, a detachment of No. 1 Special Coy. R.E. will, from positions in EAGLE TRENCH, fire Smoke and Thermit Shells on the area TINO — SPREE LANE — North of TOMBOIS TR. from ZERO plus 20 minutes to ZERO

plus 35 minutes

If the wind is unfavourable, only THERMIT will be fired

Five Mortars will be installed in DANIEL TRENCH and will fire Thermit on the area PROGGINS LANE – LOW LANE and front and support trenches between the two C.T's at intervals from ZERO plus 20 mins. to ZERO plus 45 minutes in accordance with detailed instructions communicated to No. 1 Special Coy. R.E.

5. <u>MACHINE GUN BARRAGE</u>   The advance of the Infantry will be covered by Indirect Machine Gun Barrage of 20 guns.

Dispositions of guns under the command of this Company are as under:–

BENJAMIN	– 8 guns	under	2Lt WHICHELOW
BED	– 4 "	"	Lt BEAUCHAMP
DOLEFUL	– 4 "	"	Lt. MACLELLAN
SART	– 4 "	"	Lt. STURGE

Detailed Fire Orders for above groups have already been issued to Officers concerned. Map – as per trace map issued.

6. <u>ZERO LINES</u>.   S.O.S lines of all guns will be their ZERO lines.

7. <u>ROUTINE</u>.   1 Officer per Battery and 2 men per gun will always be on duty.   Each Battery will have 2 Sentries at night and one on by day taken from the men on duty. These sentries must be on the alert for the S.O.S. Signal. The Officer on duty must be close to the Telephone.

8 (a) <u>DRESS</u> – Fighting Order.

9 <u>MAPS</u>   Officers will be in possession of
    (a) Operations Map 1/10000 – one copy.
    (b) Message Form Maps – two copies

10. <u>Aeroplanes</u> (ANTI – COUNTER ATTACK WORK)

(a) From ZERO plus 30 minutes an anti-counter attack aeroplane will be over the line, to wait for enemy troops massing for counter attack. This machine will remain up until ZERO plus 3 hours.   Other anti counter attack patrols will keep on this duty continuously throughout the day flying at about 1500 feet.

(c) The signal from anti-counter attack aeroplanes will be a smoke bomb dropped vertically over the target. The smoke bomb will burst about 100 feet below the machine into a White Parachute Flare, which descends slowly leaving a trail of brown smoke about 1 foot broad behind it.

On seeing the above signal Artillery and machine gun barrages will be opened immediately without further orders on all hostile approaches in that vicinity.

11. DIARY. Each Battery Commander will keep a record of the Operations from ZERO; giving times.

12. REPORTS. Following reports will be rendered to Advanced Coy. HQrs by 8 a.m. daily:
   Intelligence Report.
   Ammunition Expended
   Ammunition in possession

CASUALTY Report will be rendered to Adv. Coy. Hqrs by 3 p.m. daily. If a Section has at one time 25% casualties a special runner will be sent to Adv. Coy. Hqrs reporting same.

OTHER RETURNS will also be sent to Adv. Coy Hqrs, not to Coy. Hqrs. STE. EMILIE

13. RATIONS. Arrangements for rations on Z night will be notified later.

14. 164TH BRIGADE BATTLE H.Q will open at F.10.c.4.6 at 5 p.m. on Y day.

15. ADVANCED COMPANY H.Q. will open at F.16.c.35. at 5 p.m. on Y day.

16. WIRE COMMUNICATIONS
Prior to ZERO. Messages will be sent by runner. Only in cases of emergency may the wires

be used, and then only by Officers

17. FLARES and S.O.S SIGNALS.

  Flares - White

  S.O.S - Rifle Grenade bursting into
         2 GREEN and 2 WHITE.

18. SYNCHRONIZATION. Orders re this will be notified later.

19. ZERO. will be notified later.

20. ACKNOWLEDGE.

           for O.C. 165th M.G.Coy

Copy No. 1 - O.C. DOLEFUL BATTERY
   2 - O.C. BENJAMIN "
   3 - O.C. ZED "
   4 - O.C. BART "
   5 - C.O
   6 - O.C. TRANSPORT
   7 - FILE
   8 - WAR DIARY
   9 -

Vol 24

CONFIDENTIAL

War Diary
of
165th M.G. Coy
for the period
1st to 31st January 1918

Army Form C. 2118.

WAR DIARY
INTELLIGENCE SUMMARY.
(Erase heading not required.)

Instructions regarding War Diaries and Intelligence Summaries are contained in F. S. Regs., Part II. and the Staff Manual respectively. Title pages will be prepared in manuscript.

Place	Date	Hour	Summary of Events and Information	Remarks and references to Appendices
LISBOURG	1/7/18 to		Training	
PAS-16-CALAIS	31/7/18			

M. Monro Capt
for O.C. 165 MGC°Y.

WA 25

War Diary
of the
105th M.G Coy
for the period
1st to 28th February
1918.

Army Form C. 2118.

WAR DIARY
INTELLIGENCE SUMMARY.
(Erase heading not required.)

Instructions regarding War Diaries and Intelligence Summaries are contained in F. S. Regs., Part II. and the Staff Manual respectively. Title pages will be prepared in manuscript.

Place	Date	Hour	Summary of Events and Information	Remarks and references to Appendices
LISBOURG (BOMY AREA)	1/2/18 to 7/2/18		General Training	
"	8/2/18	9.30am	Company complete with Transport left LISBOURG by Route March Route under Bde Arrangements	
(BOMY AREA) CUHEM	"	12 noon	Arrived at CUHEM and BILLETED	
"	9/2/18	9.30am	Company complete with Transport left by March Route under Bde arrangements via LILLERS for	
(BUSNES AREA) LE HAMEL	9/2/18	4pm	Billets at BETHUNE in BUSNES AREA Arrived in billets at LE HAMEL	
"	10/2/18	—	Training and preparation for the Trenches	
"	11/2/18	—	Section Officers reconnoitred the forward area i.e. GIVENCHY SECTOR, held by 126th Inf Bde	
"	12/2/18	12 noon	Company complete with Transport left by March Route under Bde arrangements via CHOCQUES and BETHUNE for M.G. billets of Bde Reserve at ESSARS	
ESSARS	"	4pm	Arrived in billets at ESSARS	
"	12/2/18		Gen Training and preparation for the trenches	
"	13/2/18		Operation Order No 41 issued for Lt Cols?	

Army Form C. 2118.

WAR DIARY
or
INTELLIGENCE SUMMARY.
(Erase heading not required.)

Instructions regarding War Diaries and Intelligence
Summaries are contained in F. S. Regs., Part II.
and the Staff Manual respectively. Title pages
will be prepared in manuscript.

Place	Date	Hour	Summary of Events and Information	Remarks and references to Appendices
ESSARS	14/2/18	2.30 am	Company left by Sections to relieve 166 M.G. Coy in the line as per O.O. No 41	
		7.30 am	16 guns in the line. Transport lines at GORRE. Coy HQrs at LE PLANTIN	
FESTUBERT GIVENCHY SECTOR	"		Relief Complete. No difficulties interfered with the enroute conduct of the relief, the night being very quiet	
"	14/2/18 to 16/2/18		Situation very quiet. 3 guns used daily for indirect harrassing fire, 4500 rounds in all being fired each 24 hours.	
"	17/2/18	–	One Emma in LE PLANTIN SOUTH apparently caused by an enemy A.A. machine gun Bullet about midday	
"	20/2/18 21/2/18	9 pm–	Situation quiet.	
"	22/2/18 23/2/18	9 pm– 8.43 am	Special harrassing programme fire carried out by 7 guns at intervals throughout the night in conjunction with artillery in view of expected enemy relief.	
"	23/2/18	–	Situation quiet	
"	24/2/18	10.25 pm	Special programme above repeated.	
"	25/2/18	4.48 am		
"	26/2/18	–	Relieved in trenches by 166 M.G. Coy as per Operation Order No 42. Relief Complete at 11.30 a.m.	O.O. 42 Appx
ESSARS	"	2. pm	Company proceeded to Reserve Billets at ESSARS	

Army Form C. 2118.

WAR DIARY
or
INTELLIGENCE SUMMARY.
(Erase heading not required.)

Instructions regarding War Diaries and Intelligence Summaries are contained in F. S. Regs., Part II, and the Staff Manual respectively. Title pages will be prepared in manuscript.

Place	Date	Hour	Summary of Events and Information	Remarks and references to Appendices
ESSARS	27/9/16	5.6pm	Received orders to proceed north wds to GORRE in view of impending German attack at dawn on 28th	
GORRE	"	8pm	Arrived at GORRE + went into billets	
	28/9/16	5am	Company STOOD TO until 8am. The attack did not develop.	

M Munro Capt.
Commanding 163rd M.G. Coy

165th MACHINE GUN COY
OPERATION ORDER No 42.   COPY No 8

REF. MAPS. HAZEBROUCK 5A   23rd Feb. 1918
TRENCH MAPS.

---

1. This Company will be relieved by the 166th Machine Gun Company on the 26th Feb. 1918 in accordance with the following orders. Relief will be carried out in daylight with the exception of the 2 guns of No 2 Section in RICHMOND TR, which are to be relieved before Dawn.

2. 1 guide of No. 2 Section for RICHMOND TR guns to be at FESTUBERT CORNER at 4. a.m.
   1 guide from No. 1 Section and one guide from No. 3 Section to be at FESTUBERT CORNER at 10.30 am.
   1 guide from No. 4 Section to be at WINDY CORNER at 10.30 am; team guides for No. 1, 2 and A9, (2) positions, to meet reliefs at junction of HITCHIN ROAD, CAVAN LANE and MOAT FARM Trenches.

3. HANDING OVER. Belt boxes in addition to the usual Trench stores will be handed over and receipts obtained in the usual manner. All maps, Indirect Fire Schemes, Log books, and documents to be handed over and full particulars to be given to relieving Officer of all Defence Schemes etc.
   Receipts for Trench stores handed over to be sent to Orderly Room by 6pm on the 26th inst.

4. TRANSPORT. 1 Limber for RICHMOND TRENCH guns will be at Nos 1 & 3 Sections HQrs (FESTUBERT EAST KEEP) at 5 am. until it becomes too light, when it will move to FESTUBERT CORNER. Blankets, Officers' kits, and belt filling machines of Nos 1 and 3 Sections will be loaded on this limber.
   1 Limber for the 8 guns of Nos 1 & 3 Sections will be at FESTUBERT CORNER at 11 am.

- 2 -

1 Limber for No. 4 Section will be at WINDY CORNER at 12 noon.

1 Limber will be at Coy. HQrs at 9.30 a.m. for HQrs gear.

1 Limber will be at Coy HQrs at 11.30 a.m. for V7 and V8 guns of No. 2 Section, and any spare baggage of Coy HQrs.

<u>No PACKS</u> are to be placed on the limbers.

5. After relief Sections will proceed independently to Transport lines at GORRE, where the Company will have dinner at 1.30 p.m. and will continue the move to ESSARS during the afternoon.

6. Relief complete will be notified to Coy. HQrs. by runner as soon as possible after relief.

```
Copy No 1  - O.C. No 1 Section
  "    2  -  "    "  2    "
  "    3  -  "    "  3    "
  "    4  -  "    "  4    "
  "    5  -  "    Transport
  "    6  -  O.C. 166th M.G.Coy
  "    7  -  C.S.M.
  "    8  } WAR DIARY
  "    9  }
  "   10  -  FILE.
```

Issued @ 9.30 a.m.   for O.C. 165th Machine Gun Coy.

www.ingramcontent.com/pod-product-compliance
Lightning Source LLC
Chambersburg PA
CBHW081411160426

43193CB00013B/2154